Practice Tests Plus

B1 Preliminary
for Schools

NEW EDITION

Mark Little • Jacky Newbrook

Pearson Education Limited

KAO Two,
KAO Park,
Harlow,
Essex.
CM17 9SR
and Associated Companies throughout the world

www.english.com/practicetestsplus

First published 2019
Tenth impression 2024
ISBN 978-1-292-28216-9
Set in Helvetica Neue LT 10/12pt and Gill Sans 10/12pt
Printed Slovakia by Neografia

We are grateful to the following for permission to reproduce copyright material:
Illustration Acknowledgements
John Batten (Beehive Illustration Ltd) 20, 31, 71, 72, 90, 107, 108, 125, 143, 161, 162, 200, 201, 202, 203, 204, 206, 207; **Nigel Dobbyn** (Beehive Illustration Ltd) 30, 31, 53, 54, 71, 72, 86, 89, 90, 107, 108, 122, 125, 126, 142, 143, 161, 162.

Photo Acknowledgements
The publisher would like to thank the following for their kind permission to reproduce their photographs:
123RF.com: 80, gbh007 197, leungchopan 44; **Alamy Stock Photo:** Arco Images GmbH 196, Astrakan Images 196, Daisy-Daisy 198, Hero Images Inc. 193, Historical image collection by Bildagentur-online 68, MBI 199, Tourism Ministry / Xinhua / Alamy Live News 86; **Getty Images:** Casarsa Guru 158; **Pearson Education Ltd:** Gareth Boden 11, 44, 44, 62, 62, 80, 134, 152, 194, 195, Jon Barlow 11, 62, 116, 116, Jörg Carstensen 152, Jules Selmes 116, Miguel Domingez 44, 80, Miguel Domingues Munz 152, 197, Rob Judges 98, Sophie Bluy 152, 198, Studio 8 11, 11, 62, 80, 98, 116, 134, 152; **Shutterstock.com:** 193, 195, Ann Worthy 98, Anna Azimi 140, Anna Om 134, Apollofoto 134, Brainsil 98, Daria Chichkareva 98, Darrin Henry 134, Gladskikh Tatiana 199, Happy Together 62, Iakov Filimonov 194, Olena Zaskochenko 44, OrelPhoto 192, theerasakj 116, wizdata 11, Yan Lev 192, ZouZou 80

All other images © Pearson Education

PRACTICE TESTS PLUS
NEW EDITION RESOURCES

Where to find and how to use

Access on the **Pearson English Portal**:

	Resource	Description	When to use
AUDIO	Test 1 Training activities Tests 1–8	Audio files for Listening tests and Training.	Throughout the book.
	Audioscripts	Full scripts for the Training activities and Tests 1–8.	During or after completing any of the activities or tests as extra support.
WRITING	Sample answers	Three sample student answers for each piece of writing: – email – article – story	When Test 1 training is complete, use with Test 2 Writing. Sample student answers are written using Test 2 questions, the worksheets aim to help students write good answers to these questions.
	Examiner feedback for each sample answer	Examiner feedback on the three sample student answers for each piece of writing: – email – article – story	
	Student activity worksheet by writing genre	Worksheet 1 – email Worksheet 2 – article Worksheet 3 – story Page 1 – focuses on sample answers and examiner feedback on these to help students understand what makes a 'good' answer. Page 2 – builds process writing skills and gives additional language input.	
SPEAKING	Videos	Speaking test About the exam Candidate feedback Frequently asked questions Examiner feedback	Watch with or without the worksheets described below.
	Student activity Worksheets	Worksheet 1 – focus on test format Worksheet 2 – focus on Part 1 Worksheet 3 – focus on Part 2 Worksheet 4 – focus on Part 3 Worksheet 5 – focus on Part 4 Page 1 – focuses on real students' answers and what makes a good response. Page 2 – focuses on building confidence and useful language for the test.	Worksheet 1 – use with *About the exam* video Worksheet 2 – use with *Speaking test video Part 1* Worksheet 3 – use with *Speaking test video Part 2* Worksheet 4 – use with *Speaking test video Part 3* Worksheet 5 – use with *Speaking test video Part 4*
	Video transcripts	Speaking test About the exam Candidates' feedback Frequently asked questions Examiner feedback	During or after watching any of the videos as extra support.
VOCABULARY MAPS	Vocabulary maps for over 20 topics	Vocabulary items organised by topic to help students extend their vocabulary.	Find the matching topic and use with any test to build vocabulary.

Access on the **Pearson English App**:

	Resource	Description	When to use
AUDIO	Test 1 Training activities Tests 1–8	Audio files for Listening tests and Training activities.	Throughout the book.
SPEAKING	Videos	Speaking test About the exam Candidate feedback Frequently asked questions Examiner feedback	Watch with or without the speaking test worksheets.
VOCABULARY BUILDING PRACTICE	Topic-based vocabulary practice	Each topic includes a practice exercise on meaning and one on use.	Find the matching topic and use with any test to build vocabulary.

EXAM OVERVIEW

The **Cambridge Preliminary English Test for Schools**, also known as **PETfS**, is made up of **four papers**, each testing a different area of ability in English. The Reading, Writing, Listening and Speaking papers each carry 25% of the marks. There are five grades: A, B and C are pass grades, D and E are fail grades. Candidates also receive a numerical score on the Cambridge Scale for each of the four skills.

Reading   45 minutes

Writing   45 minutes

Listening   30 minutes (approximately)

Speaking   12 minutes (approximately) for each pair of students.

Paper	Format	Task Focus
Reading 6 tasks, 32 questions	Part 1: 5 short texts, multiple choice, 5 questions, 3 options each.	Understanding short messages of different types.
	Part 2: Match 5 descriptions of people with 8 short texts.	Reading for specific information and detailed comprehension.
	Part 3: Longer text, multiple choice, 5 questions, 4 options.	Reading for gist, global and detailed meaning, attitude, opinions and feelings.
	Part 4: Gapped text, choose correct sentences to put in gaps, 5 gaps, 8 options.	Reading to understand gist and text structure.
	Part 5: Gap fill text, choose missing words, 6 questions, 4 options.	Reading for specific meaning (vocabulary).
	Part 6: Open gap fill, write words in the gaps, 6 questions.	Reading for specific meaning (grammar).
Writing 3 tasks, 2 questions	Part 1: Write an email in response to information given (about 100 words).	Focus on writing a short informative text using appropriate language.
	Part 2: Write either an article or a story on the topic given (about 100 words).	Focus on writing a short creative or factual text using appropriate language.
Listening 4 tasks, 25 questions	Part 1: Multiple choice, 7 short recordings, 3 picture options.	Listening for specific information.
	Part 2: Multiple choice, 6 short recordings, 3 options.	Listening for attitudes and opinions.
	Part 3: Gap fill. Write 1 or 2 words in 6 gaps in a short text about the recording.	Listening for specific information.
	Part 4: Multiple choice, 6 questions, 3 options.	Listening for specific information, detailed meaning, attitudes and opinions.
Speaking 4 tasks	Part 1: Introductory phase, examiner-led conversation.	Candidates show ability to use general interactional and social language.
	Part 2: Individual long turn. Visual prompts.	Describing photographs and managing discourse, using appropriate vocabulary in a longer turn.
	Part 3: Collaborative task. Visual prompts.	Using functional language to make and respond to suggestions, discuss alternatives, make recommendations and negotiate agreement.
	Part 4: Discussion with another candidate.	Talking about likes/dislikes, preferences, habits, opinions and agreeing/disagreeing. Linked to collaborative task in Part 3.

CONTENTS

OVERVIEW
TEST 1: READING

About the paper

There are six parts. You read both short and long texts and answer different types of questions. In Parts 1–3, you have to show that you can read and completely understand the texts. In Parts 4–6, you have to both read the texts and show that you can use language correctly.

The test lasts 45 minutes. This includes the time you spend writing your answers on the separate answer sheet.

For Parts 1–6, there is one mark for each correct answer.

How to do the paper

Part 1

In Part 1, you read five short texts on different topics. Some of the texts are notices you might see in different places. Others might be messages, such as emails, phone messages and so on. There is one multiple-choice question about each text. Each multiple-choice question has three options (**A**, **B** and **C**). You have to choose the option which is closest to the meaning of the text.

Part 2

In Part 2, you read eight short texts. They are all on the same topic and contain similar ideas and information. For example, you could read eight reviews of websites or information about eight different courses or places. You also have to read information about five people. You have to decide which person matches each short text. For example, you might need to decide which website each person would find most useful or which course they should do.

Part 3

In Part 3, you read one longer text. This might be about a person, an event or something else. You have to answer five multiple-choice questions about the text. Each multiple-choice question has four options (**A**, **B**, **C** and **D**). The questions are about details in the text, as well as about feelings, attitudes and opinions expressed by the writer or a person in the text.

Part 4

In Part 4, you read one long text about an interesting person, place or event. This time, five sentences are missing from the text. After the text, there is a list of eight sentences (**A–H**). You have to choose the five missing sentences and decide which one fits each gap. In this way, you show that you can use reference words like pronouns and other vocabulary to link together the ideas in a text.

Part 5

In Part 5, you read one short text. Six words are missing from the text. For each missing word, there is a multiple-choice question, which gives you four possible words to use in the gap. You have to choose the best word (**A**, **B**, **C** or **D**). You look at the words before and after the gap to help you choose the best one. In this way, you show your understanding of vocabulary and how words are used together in a text.

Part 6

In Part 6, you read one short text. Six words are missing from the text. You have to think of the missing word yourself to fill each gap. In this part, the missing words are mostly grammatical words like pronouns, prepositions and so on. By writing the correct word, you show that you understand how to use grammatical words to write good sentences.

Focus on the instructions

1 Look at the exam task on pages 8 and 9.

  a How many questions do you have to answer?

  b What do you have to decide?

  c How many options do you have to choose from for each question?

2 Look at this example below. What kind of text is it?

  a a notice   **b** an email   **c** a note

> Mum,
>
> Please can you pick up the book I ordered from the bookshop when you go shopping this afternoon? I've already paid for it so there's no need to give them any money.
>
> Thanks!
>
> Max

3 Where might you see it?

4 What does the note say?

  a Max will give his mum some money for the book this afternoon.

  b Max would like his mum to collect a book for him later today.

  c Max wants his mum to take him to the bookshop when she goes shopping.

5 The correct answer to question **4** above is **b**. In the text, underline the words which mean the same as *collect* and *later today*.

6 Why is option **a** in question **4** wrong? Is Max going to give his mum some money? Why not?

7 Why is option **c** wrong? Does Max want to go with his mum? How do you know?

Focus on the questions

1 Look at question **1** on page 8. What kind of text is this?

  a a sign   **b** a note   **c** a label

2 Now answer these questions about question **1**.

  a Where might you see it?

  b What might you do before you see it?

  c Underline the words in options **A**, **B** and **C** which have the same meaning as *Take a seat*.

  d Underline the words in options **A**, **B** and **C** which have the same meaning as *choose what you'd like*.

  e Why is option **C** wrong?

3 Look at question **2**. Where might you see this kind of text?

4 Now answer these questions about question **2**.

  a Do members of the film club need to see the school secretary?

  b What should members talk to Mr Tanner about?

5 Look at question **3**. What kind of text is this?

  a a note   **b** a text message   **c** an email

6 Answer these questions about question **3**.

  a What do you think is the relationship between Vivian and Pat?

  b Which of these sentences says what Vivian needs to do now?

    i Tell Pat whether she is still vegetarian or not.

    ii Ask Pat what food she should take to the party.

7 Look at question **4**. Where might you see a text like this?

8 Now answer these questions about question **4**.

  a Does Angela mention that Melissa should help her look for the lost phone?

  b Look at option **B**. Is it correct? Why?

  c Option **C** is wrong. What does the text say about who is going to phone Valerie?

9 Look at question **5**. What kind of text is this?

  a an email   **b** a note   **c** a label

10 Answer these questions about question **5**.

  a Who is unwell?

  b Where are Billy and Charlie going to meet tonight?

  c What are they going to do together?

Part 1

Questions 1 – 5

For each question, choose the correct answer.

___

1

Riverside Café

Take a seat and choose what you'd like from our menu. A waiter will come to your table shortly.

Customers should

A   wait until a member of staff tells them where they can sit.

B   find a table before deciding what to have and placing their order.

C   choose what to eat and drink then find a seat at a table.

2

School Film Club

This week's film, *Star Battle*, is at 4 p.m. on Wednesday in the hall. Suggestions for future films to Mr Tanner, please.

New members welcome.

See the school secretary for membership details.

A   Anyone wanting to join the film club should contact the school secretary.

B   Club members must tell the school secretary if they want to see *Star Battle*.

C   New members should ask Mr Tanner about what films are showing in the future.

3

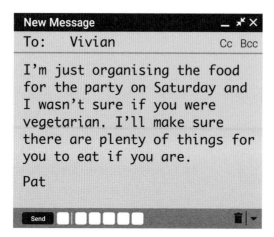

New Message

To: Vivian   Cc Bcc

I'm just organising the food for the party on Saturday and I wasn't sure if you were vegetarian. I'll make sure there are plenty of things for you to eat if you are.

Pat

Send

A   Pat is suggesting that Vivian helps her prepare some vegetarian food for the party.

B   Pat is reminding Vivian to bring some vegetarian food to the party on Saturday.

C   Pat is checking whether Vivian is vegetarian so she can provide the right party food.

4

> **Melissa**
> I've got a different phone!
> I accidentally left mine
> somewhere and can't find it.
> Could you text me Valerie's
> number as I no longer have
> it and need to ring her?
> Angela

‹ Back   Contacts

Angela wants Melissa to

A   help her look for a phone that she recently lost.

B   send her the contact details of a friend.

C   phone a friend for her as she's lost her number.

5

> Charlie
> You know you'd planned to go to
> Billy's tonight to practise playing the
> guitar together? His mum phoned to
> say she's not well so I've said Billy can
> come here instead.
> Dad

A   Billy is unwell so Charlie can't go to his house to practise tonight.

B   Charlie needs to finish his guitar practice before going to Billy's house.

C   Charlie's dad has invited Billy to their house to practise tonight.

PART 2: TRAINING

Focus on the instructions

1 Look at the exam task on pages 11 and 12.

   a How many questions do you need to answer?

   b How many options are there to choose from for each question?

   c What do all the people want?

   d What are the descriptions for?

   e What do you need to decide?

Focus on the questions

1 Read text **6** and answer these questions.

   a What does Li want to find out about?

   b What does Li like learning about?

   c What does Li want advice about?

   d Underline the three parts of the text about Li that contain your answers to questions **1–3**.

2 Now read text **7** and answer these questions.

   a Edwin wants to find out more about animals that live in which two places?

   b What else would he like the documentaries to include?

   c Underline the three parts of the text about Edwin that contain your answers to questions **a** and **b**.

3 Read text **8** and answer these questions.

   a What does Ulrika want to learn about?

   b Where does she want the documentaries to be filmed?

   c What does she want to know?

   d Underline the three parts of the text about Ulrika that contain your answers to questions **a–c**.

4 Read text **9** and answer these questions.

   a What does Marco want to find out about?

   b What would he like the series to show?

   c What kind of species does he want to see?

   d Underline the three parts of the text about Marco that contain your answers to questions **a–c**.

5 Read text **10** and answer these questions.

   a Who does Stacey want the documentaries to be presented by?

   b What does she enjoy seeing in documentaries?

   c What does she want to find out?

   d Underline the three parts of the text about Stacey that contain your answers to questions **a–c**.

6 Look again at text **6**. These are words about Li's interests: *rare animals, deserts, helping the environment.* Underline words about these things in texts **A–H**.

7 In which text have you underlined more words than in the other texts?

8 Does this text contain information about the three things that Li wants?

9 Read text **6** again. Which of the texts **A–H** talks the most about Li's interests?

10 Look at the important information you underlined in texts **6–10** again.

   • Read through the descriptions **A–H**.

   • Underline the words about the information you underlined in texts **6–10**.

   • Why are the following answers not correct?

   a 8 F

   b 9 B

   c 10 E

11 Now do the exam task for Part 2.

Questions 6 – 10

For each question, choose the correct answer.

The young people below all want to watch a documentary series about the natural world.

On page 12 there are descriptions of eight documentary series.

Decide which series would be most suitable for the people below.

6  Li is doing a project on rare animals and would like to see a series that includes information about them. She loves learning about deserts and would also like advice about helping the environment.

7  Edwin is keen to know more about animals that live in cold places. He'd like to find out about what lives on beaches and coasts, and he likes programmes with soundtracks by famous musicians.

8  Ulrika likes learning about nature in mountain ranges and would prefer to see a series that was filmed around the world. She wants to know how different landscapes were formed.

9  Marco would love to find out how humans are affecting wildlife. He'd like the series to show life in jungles, including species that no one has filmed before.

10  Stacey is looking for a series that's presented by a famous scientist. She enjoys seeing animals that live in the sea and wants to find out how climate affects animals that live in different places.

Nature documentary series

A Watch Nature

The *Watch Nature* team spent two years filming in and around the African rainforest. Presented by famous biology expert Magnus Green, the series focuses as much on people's influence on the wildlife as on the lives of the creatures themselves. Several of the animals appear for the first time on film.

B Wild World

There's film of some unusual sea creatures in this fantastic series. Some of the species are shown for the first time on film. There are amazing pictures of extremely rare sharks swimming under ice near Greenland. The series was filmed in all of the world's oceans.

C Nature Planet

With an amazing soundtrack provided by famous guitarist Stella Murray, *Nature Planet* focuses on species that live in the driest places on Earth and whose numbers are so low they're in danger of disappearing altogether. It includes information on what we can all do to care more for the natural world.

D Our Planet

From the driest desert to the deepest ocean, this series has everything. Recorded in over fifty countries, *Our Planet* explains how the geography of each region ended up being so different, as well as showing us the lives of the animals living there. The two programmes about life in the world's highest peaks are not to be missed.

E Fragile Earth

With a focus on how people and climate change are affecting nature worldwide, this series is not only beautiful to look at, but sounds great too, with music provided by the world-famous Capital Orchestra. It shows the damage humans are doing but also suggests solutions.

F Third Planet from the Sun

You're sure to have seen Dr Joyce Angel on TV before. In this series, the university physics professor explains why weather, more than anything else, influences what lives in each region. See how creatures in the world's oceans and mountain ranges are affected by small changes in temperature.

G Channel Nature

This wonderful series shows how several major landscapes were created. With beautiful music provided by well-known singers George and Hans Severin, we follow the lives of animals that make their homes on shores around the world. Several programmes look at how the wildlife of the Antarctic survives the freezing temperatures there.

H Earth Central

Filmed on all seven of the world's continents, *Earth Central* is science researcher and presenter Larry Halliwell's latest series. We follow a family of monkeys in the jungle in one of the episodes, and discover how animals that live on beaches are affected by large numbers of people using them during the summer in another.

Focus on the instructions

1 Look at the exam task on pages 14 and 15.

  a What do you have to read?

  b What do you have to do?

  c How many questions are there?

  d How many options are there for each question?

2 Read the text quickly and answer the questions.

  a What activity is the writer mainly talking about?

  b How did Daniella first become interested in furniture design?

  c What problems did Daniella have with the first table she made?

  d What two businesses does Daniella mention?

  e What had Daniella taken part in recently?

Focus on the questions

1 Read questions **11–15** on page 15. Choose the correct words to complete these statements. The information in brackets will help you.

  a Question **11** asks about the *writer's family / the writer*.
    (This is always a question about detail, attitude, feeling or opinion.)

  b Question **12** asks about *the first furniture the writer made / the furniture the writer makes now*.
    (This is always a question about detail, attitude, feeling or opinion.)

  c Question **13** asks about *opinion / detail*.
    (This is always a question about detail, attitude, feeling or opinion.)

  d Question **14** asks about *feeling / opinion*.
    (This is always a question about detail, attitude, feeling or opinion.)

  e Question **15** asks about what the writer *has said / is likely to say*.
    (This is always a question which asks about information from several different parts of the text.)

2 Look at these sentences from the text. Put them in the order in which they appear.

  a *Judging by how many items Daniella sold, they thought it was pretty good.*

  b *Since that day, she's been making furniture.*

  c *Rather than worrying about this, Daniella was excited by the opportunity.*

  d *I was pleased with the quality of my work, though.*

  e *One of the organisers had bought one of my pieces off the internet.*

3 Now read question **11** again and look at options **A–D**.

  A Does the writer tell us that her interest came from watching online films?

  B Does the writer show us that her interest came from helping her parents make furniture?

  C Does the writer suggest that her interest came from visiting furniture shops?

  D Does the writer say that her interest came from somewhere she visited on a school trip?

4 In question **12** the correct answer is **C**. Can you underline the part of the text that includes this information?

5 In question **13** the correct answer is **B**. Can you underline the part of the text that includes this information?

6 In question **14** the correct answer is **A**. What tells you that Daniella was 'surprised' in the text?

7 In question **15** the correct answer is **B**. Can you underline the parts of the text that contain this information? Why are options **A**, **C** and **D** wrong?

Questions 11 – 15

For each question, choose the correct answer.

The Teenage Furniture Designer
15-year-old Daniella Hudson recently took part in her first design show.

Daniella Hudson grew up in a very creative family. 'Mum and dad made all our furniture,' she says. 'Not because we couldn't afford it: they just preferred making stuff to buying it. So visits to city furniture shops nearby just weren't part of my childhood.' When Daniella visited a design exhibition with her class at the age of ten, she realised she wanted to follow her parents' example. 'There were so many different styles of tables and chairs there!' she says. Since that day, she's been making furniture. 'I've learnt by giving mum and dad a hand, and through watching videos on the internet.'

Her first piece was a table, made soon after visiting the exhibition, and similar to one she'd seen there. 'They had furniture from the last hundred years, and I copied a 1920s design,' comments Daniella. 'Unfortunately, no one has wanted tables like that for years. I was pleased with the quality of my work, though. I've painted it recently because the wood I chose originally was too dark.'

Daniella started selling her furniture at a local market. 'I spend most of my free time inside so this gave me the chance to get some fresh air and find out what people thought about my designs.' Judging by how many items Daniella sold, they thought it was pretty good. 'Eventually, I had to give up,' says Daniella. 'I'd also started an internet business, which was doing so well it was taking up every spare minute I had. The market closed down just after that anyway.'

Recently, Daniella was asked to take part in a local design show. 'One of the organisers had bought one of my pieces off the internet. I couldn't believe it when she told me there'd be a thousand visitors,' she comments. Rather than worrying about this, Daniella was excited by the opportunity. 'I was amazed she thought my work was good enough,' Daniella says. 'I had little idea what visitors would think about it. My furniture is quite different from the designers whose work I've seen in magazines – mine is more traditional.' But Daniella received lots of orders at the show and the future is looking bright for this young design star.

11 Daniella's interest in creating furniture came from

    A   watching online films of how to make furniture.

    B   helping her parents create their own furniture.

    C   visiting furniture shops in a city near her home.

    D   seeing a huge range of furniture on a school trip.

12 What does Daniella say about the first item of furniture she made?

    A   The design she chose was original.

    B   She still likes the colour she used.

    C   It wasn't a fashionable piece.

    D   It wasn't very well-made.

13 Why did Daniella stop selling her furniture at a market?

    A   Too few people were buying it.

    B   She no longer had enough time.

    C   She didn't like working outdoors.

    D   The market closed down.

14 When Daniella was invited to her first design show, she felt

    A   surprised that someone was impressed by her furniture.

    B   confident her designs would be popular.

    C   anxious about how many people would be there.

    D   curious about seeing other designers' work.

15 What would Daniella say in advertising material for her company?

A
> I'm a young furniture designer, whose work has appeared in several design shows and is sold in many city furniture shops.

B
> I've created furniture since I was just ten years old. Many of the thousand visitors to a recent design show liked my work.

C
> After starting my business at a local market, I've finally opened my own store in a local city.

D
> I'm very interested in the history of furniture but my designs are very modern and use the latest techniques.

PART 4: TRAINING

Focus on the instructions

1 Look at the exam task on pages 17 and 18.

a What do you have to read?

b What do you have to do?

c How many gaps are there?

d How many sentences are there?

e Do you have to use all the sentences?

2 Read the text quickly. What is it about?

3 Match the five paragraphs in the text to the following topics.

a The arrival of ice cream in England

b The development of freezers

c When and where ice cream was first made

d The appearance of ice cream cones

e The arrival of ice cream in Europe

Focus on the questions

1 Read the text again carefully and decide which of the sentences **A–H** should fill each gap.

2 Now answer these questions about questions **16–20**.

a In question **16** the correct answer is **C**. Underline the words in the text before the gap which *it* refers to.

b Is either of the ingredients mentioned in sentence **C** *milk* or *cream*?

c In question **17** the correct answer is **H**. Does *then* in sentence **H** mean the same thing as *in the past* or *next*?

d Underline the words in the text before the gap which *He* in sentence **H** refers to.

e In question **18** the correct answer is **A**. Underline the words in the text before the gap which *he* in sentence **A** refers to.

f Underline the words in the text after the gap which refer to keeping a secret.

g In question **19** the correct answer is **F**. Does *therefore* in sentence **F** mean the same things as *after* or *as a result*?

h Underline the words in the text before the gap which *They* in sentence **F** refers to.

i In question **20** the correct answer is **D**. Underline the words in the text before the gap which *one* in sentence **D** refers to.

j Does the use of *also* in the sentence after the gap mean you are looking for another advantage of electric freezers or another way of keeping ice cream cold?

Focus on the language

1 Read these sentences and think about the connection between them. Choose the correct option to complete the second sentence.

a The children were hungry after the journey and wanted to eat as soon as they arrived. *Because / So* it was lucky that their grandparents *cooked / had cooked* a big meal for them.

b The café where he was writing his essay was very noisy. *That's why / That's how* he went to the library to write it *also / instead*.

c My family gave me a camera for my birthday. *It / They* took me out for dinner *too / now*.

d They don't need to get up early tomorrow. *For example / After all*, they're *on holiday / at school*.

e There were a lot of interesting places to see on the island. *However / Finally*, many of *these / theirs* were difficult to reach by car.

f There are lots of useful *jobs / projects* that you could do when you're older. *For instance / As a result*, you could become a nurse or a firefighter.

Part 4

Questions 16 – 20

Five sentences have been removed from the text below.

For each question, choose the correct answer.

There are three extra sentences which you do not need to use.

The History of Ice Cream

You might think ice cream is a modern kind of food, but actually, ice cream was probably first eaten in China over 2000 years ago. It was made from a mixture of rice and milk, and was frozen using snow. In Europe around 2000 years ago, Roman leaders also enjoyed a type of frozen dessert. **16** [ ] It wasn't true ice cream, though, as it had no milk or cream in it.

Italian explorer Marco Polo spent a lot of time in China during the late thirteenth century. People believe that he saw ice cream being made while he was on his travels there. **17** [ ] This was the first time true ice cream was made in Europe. Perhaps this is why Italians are considered the European masters of ice-cream making: they have had more time than other countries to practise the recipe!

In the seventeenth century, King Charles I of England was introduced to the pleasures of ice cream by his new French chef. He was so amazed by its beautiful taste that he immediately offered the chef £500 a year (worth around £100 000 in today's money!). This wasn't just for him to make Charles lots more ice cream. **18** [ ] No one knows if he ever told anyone!

Ice cream cones are a popular way to serve ice cream. They're a convenient way to hold ice cream while you eat it and there's no waste at all because you eat the container along with the ice cream. **19** [ ] It's believed they were invented in 1904 in the USA.

Ice cream very quickly became even more popular in the middle of the twentieth century. At this time, the first electric freezers became available to the public. **20** [ ] They also allowed greater access to ice cream to those living in hot climates.

A   It was so he kept the recipe a secret too.

B   Although they found there was already plenty available across Europe.

C   The simple recipe for it contained only snow and fruit.

D   Owning one meant you could then keep ice cream at home.

E   As it was so cold, there was no need to have a fridge to keep it in.

F   They're therefore environmentally friendly as well as tasty.

G   These were usually served to him in a small bowl of some sort.

H   He then brought the recipe for it back home when he returned.

PART 5: TRAINING

Focus on the instructions

1 Look at the exam task on page 20.

  a What do you have to read?

  b How many questions are there?

  c What do you have to choose?

  d How many options do you have to choose from for each question?

2 Read the text on page 20 and answer these questions.

  a Is it factual or is it a story?

  b Is it difficult to understand what the text is about?

  c Are there any questions about the meaning of the text?

  d Is it a long text or a short text?

Focus on the questions

1 Now look at questions **21–26** on page 20. Answer these questions about them.

  a Look at question **21**. What do you call the line between two countries or states? Which word is correct here?

  b In question **22** which verb do we use to describe where a region or place is?

  c Look at question **23**. What do we use square kilometres and square metres to measure?

  d In question **24** notice the word *tiny* just after the gap. Which of the possible answers goes with this extreme adjective to mean 'very'?

  e In question **25** which word means the same as *stop someone doing something*?

  f Look at question **26**. You need to choose an adjective that means that something happens very often. Which one is it?

Focus on the language

1 Look at the options **A–D** for questions **21–26** again. Now choose one of the options from each question to complete the sentences below.

  a Be careful because your glass is close to the .... of the table. (Question **21**)

  b My mum sometimes .... really late at work. (Question **22**)

  c The first .... of an essay is usually an introduction. (Question **23**)

  d She lost the competition, even though she was .... the best singer. (Question **24**)

  e She .... me every time I start talking! (Question **25**)

  f I'm sure we've met before – your face looks very .... (Question **26**)

Part 5

Questions 21 – 26

For each question, choose the correct answer.

Alaska

Alaska is the largest of the fifty states that make up the USA. Although it is part of the United States, it doesn't actually have a land **(21)**.................... with any of the other forty-nine states. It actually **(22)**.................... between Canada to the east and the Pacific and Arctic Oceans to the south, west and north. It has a total **(23)**............... of over 1.7 million square kilometres.

Although Alaska is huge, its population is **(24)**............... tiny, with well under a million people living in this enormous state. What probably **(25)**.................. a greater number of people from wanting to move there is the climate. In the state's largest city, Anchorage, the maximum daily temperature in summer is only around 18 °C. In many parts of the state, temperatures of –20 °C are **(26)**............... in winter.

21	**A**	limit	**B**	border	**C**	edge	**D**	side
22	**A**	rests	**B**	stays	**C**	remains	**D**	lies
23	**A**	area	**B**	region	**C**	section	**D**	district
24	**A**	certainly	**B**	totally	**C**	absolutely	**D**	definitely
25	**A**	interrupts	**B**	ends	**C**	avoids	**D**	prevents
26	**A**	common	**B**	natural	**C**	familiar	**D**	regular

PART 6: TRAINING

Focus on the instructions

1   Look at the exam task on page 22.
  a What do you have to read?
  b How many questions are there?
  c What do you have to do?
  d How many words can you choose for each gap?
  e How many options are there for each gap?

2   Read the text on page 22 and answer these questions.
  a What kind of text is it?
  b Is it difficult to understand what the text is about?
  c Are there any questions about the meaning of the text?
  d Is it a long text or a short text?
  e What kind of words are missing?

Focus on the questions

1   Look at question **27**. Which kind of word is missing? Answer these questions to help you decide.
  a Which words can go between *I* and a verb ending in *–ing*, like *wondering*?
  b What tense do you think the verb is in: past, present or future?
  c What word should you therefore put in the phrase *I* .... *wondering*?

2   Look at question **28**. Which word is sometimes used as a subject before *is*, *was*, *are* or *were* when you are describing a place or an event?

3   In question **29** which word completes the short phrase for saying how many of the fireworks were loud?

4   Look at question **30**.
  a What is the phrase .... *soon as* about here: comparing things, times or something else?
  b What word can you put in the phrase .... *soon as* so that it means *immediately*?

5   Look at question **31**. Which word completes the short phrase that's used to introduce some information?

6   In question **32** what word goes after *how* to ask or talk about a number?

Focus on the language

1   Look at some more examples of the type of words that are often tested in Part 6. Complete each sentence with one word in each gap. Remember to look at the words before and after the gaps carefully.
  a This box is .... heavy for me to carry – I can't even pick it up!
  b That mountain is .... high that it's very difficult to climb.
  c I haven't seen Liz .... March, when she moved to Manchester.
  d *Highlight* is the .... interesting book I've ever read.
  e I hate travelling .... train but my sister loves it.
  f He couldn't decide whether to stay at home .... go out with his friends.
  g This sweater doesn't cost as .... as that one.
  h My cousin invited his friends to the party as .... as all his family.
  i The people .... live next door are very friendly.
  j .... I enjoyed most about the film was the music.

Questions 27 – 32

For each question, write the correct answer.

Write **one** word for each gap.

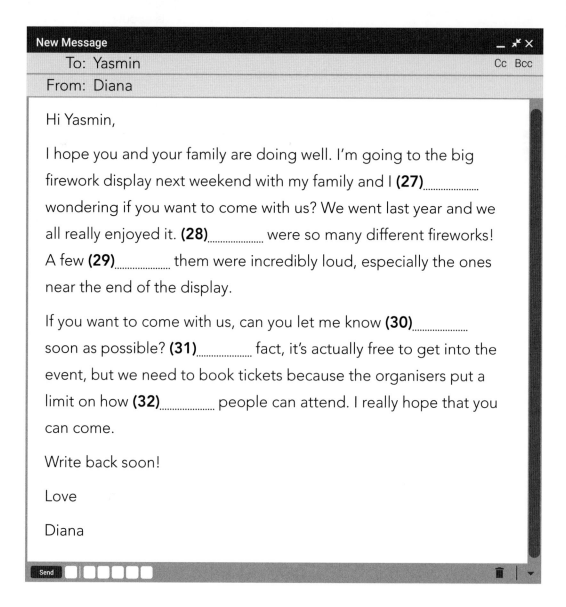

New Message   — ⤢ ✕

To: Yasmin   Cc Bcc

From: Diana

Hi Yasmin,

I hope you and your family are doing well. I'm going to the big firework display next weekend with my family and I **(27)**............... wondering if you want to come with us? We went last year and we all really enjoyed it. **(28)**............... were so many different fireworks! A few **(29)**............... them were incredibly loud, especially the ones near the end of the display.

If you want to come with us, can you let me know **(30)**............... soon as possible? **(31)**............... fact, it's actually free to get into the event, but we need to book tickets because the organisers put a limit on how **(32)**............... people can attend. I really hope that you can come.

Write back soon!

Love

Diana

Send ☐☐☐☐☐☐   🗑 | ▾

About the paper

There are two parts in the Writing test and you must write two pieces. The first is always an email (Part 1). The second is a story or an article (Part 2). In Part 2 you choose which type of text you want to write.

You have 45 minutes to do the Writing test, so you have 20–25 minutes for each part. This includes the time to read the tasks and think about them before you start writing, and the time to decide which task to choose in Part 2.

You get the same number of marks in Part 1 and in Part 2, so you must try to do both well. The examiner will give you good marks if:

• you have included all the information

• your writing is clear and easy to follow and understand

• you have used some good language, with good spelling and punctuation.

How to do the paper

Part 1

In Part 1, there is only one task, which you must do. On the page you will see an email from a friend, a teacher or another English-speaking person, with four notes around it. Your task is to write an **email** replying to this person, using all the notes. You should write about 100 words.

Part 2

In Part 2, there is a choice between two tasks: a **story** or an **article**. You must choose one of them and write about 100 words. For the story, you are given the first sentence, which is the beginning of the story. For the article, you are given the title and also some questions that you must answer.

How do I decide what to choose in Part 2?

Don't waste too much time deciding. Choose the one you like most! Think about these things to help you decide.

• Do I like the topic of the article?

• Do I understand what I need to write about?

• Can I think of some ideas to make the article interesting?

• Do I know some interesting vocabulary I can use?

• Do I like the way the story begins?

• Do I have some good ideas to make my story interesting?

• Do I know some interesting vocabulary I can use?

See **WRITING BANK** for useful language and practice
See **GRAMMAR BANK** for reference and practice

Focus on the instructions

1   Look at the exam task on page 25.

   a Do you have to do this question or can you choose to do a different one?

   b What are you going to write?

   c Who are you going to write to?

   d How many things do you need to write about?

   e How many words do you need to write?

Focus on the questions

1   Read question 1 and follow these steps to help plan your answer.

- Why are you writing this email?
- What will you say first in the email?
- How did you know that Max loves tennis? What reason could you give?
- What do you need to write about next?
- What do you need to describe for the third point?
- Why might there not be a good place to eat near the tennis club?

2   Look at your answers to exercise 1. Write a sentence for each of the points. Use these to help you write your answer for Part 1.

3   Read a student's answer to question **1** on page 25. Choose the correct answer **A** or **B** to complete it.

1	**A** Bye	**B** Hi
2	**A** told	**B** said
3	**A** told	**B** said
4	**A** could	**B** would
5	**A** Could	**B** Would
6	**A** need	**B** can
7	**A** need	**B** can
8	**A** go	**B** going

---

(1).................... Max

Your brother **(2)**.................... me that you really like tennis actually. He **(3)**.................... that you watch it on TV all the time.

I **(4)**.................... go on Sunday instead of Saturday.

(5).................... that be good for you too?

You **(6)**.................... wear any kind of shorts and T-shirt that you want at the club, but you **(7)**.................... to make sure that you wear proper tennis shoes.

I don't know a cafe near the club, no, but there's one in Brook Street. It has great sandwiches and cakes! How about **(8)**.................... there?

See you at the weekend,

Darren

Focus on the language

1   Match the first parts of sentences **1–6** with the second parts **A–F**.

  1 I'd love to go

  2 There are no restaurants or cafés

  3 Why don't we go into town and

  4 I recommend that you bring

  5 I remember you said that you had spent

  6 I'm free on Saturday so

  A near the club.

  B the weekend watching tennis on TV.

  C find somewhere to eat there?

  D maybe we could play then instead.

  E for something to eat afterwards.

  F your own racket and some balls too.

Part I

You **must** answer this question.

Write your answer in about **100 words**.

_____

Question 1

Read this email from your English-speaking friend Max and the notes you have made.

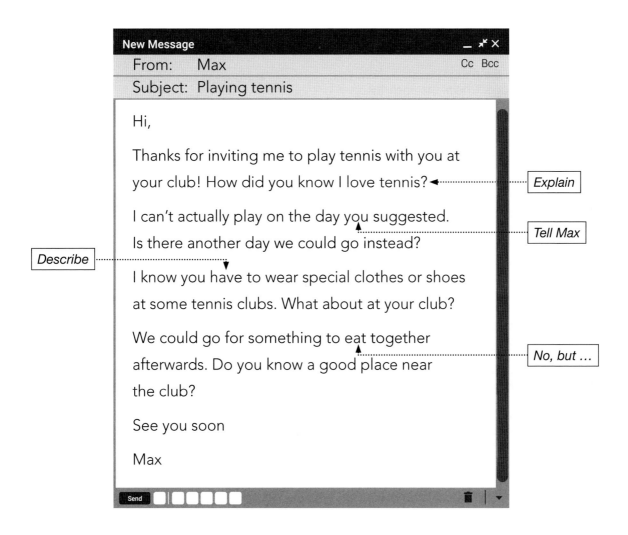

New Message — ⤢ ✕

From: Max   Cc Bcc

Subject: Playing tennis

Hi,

Thanks for inviting me to play tennis with you at your club! How did you know I love tennis? ◄········ *Explain*

I can't actually play on the day you suggested. Is there another day we could go instead? ········· *Tell Max*

Describe ········ I know you have to wear special clothes or shoes at some tennis clubs. What about at your club?

We could go for something to eat together afterwards. Do you know a good place near the club? ········· *No, but …*

See you soon

Max

Send ▢▯▢▢▢▢▢   🗑 | ▼

Write your **email** to Max using **all the notes**.

PART 2: TRAINING

Focus on the instructions

1 Look at the exam task on page 27.

   a How many questions are there in this part of the exam?

   b How many questions must you answer?

   c How many words do you need to write?

   d Where do you write your answer?

Focus on the questions

1 Read question **2** and follow these steps to help plan your answer.

- Make a list of the things you do to help you learn a language. Check the spellings.
- Decide if you think having classes is better than visiting a country where the language is spoken. Write down two or three reasons to support your opinion.
- Make a list of advantages of each way of learning a language.
- Make a list of disadvantages of each way of learning a language.

2 Now read question **3** and follow these steps.

- Look at the sentence given and think of a story you could write.

- What happens in the second sentence?
- What will happen after that?
- How will your story end?
- Write down five or six useful words and phrases that you can use in your story.

3 Look at your notes for exercises 2 and 3 above and choose which question you will answer. Think about these things.

- Do you have enough ideas for the article? Do you know all the vocabulary you'll need? Can you write 100 words?
- Do you have enough ideas for the story? Do you know all the vocabulary you'll need? Can you write 100 words?
- Which of the questions seems easier to you?

Focus on the language

1 Read a student's answer to question **2**. Complete it with the words and phrases from the box.

if you live you'll improve a week	
learning in class however you can't really	

Learning a language

Is the best way to learn a language by going to classes or by going to a country where the language is spoken? Whatever method you choose, it will take time and practice.

(1)_____ learn a language well just by going on holiday somewhere because it isn't long enough. **(2)**_____ there for several months, though, you'll use the language every day and **(3)**_____ very quickly.

If this isn't possible, then **(4)**_____ with a teacher will help. **(5)**_____, you will probably only practise for two or three hours **(6)**_____ . Therefore, learning a language in this way will take longer.

2 Read a student's answer to question **3**. Complete it with the words and phrases from the box.

started throwing fortunately were going to	
with the ball kicked the ball it was amazing	

As they set off on their bikes, they knew they were going to have an exciting day. Andrew and Richard had loads of things to eat and drink because they **(1)**_____ spend a day at the beach.

When they arrived, they started playing football. Richard accidentally **(2)**_____ into the sea and ran in to get it. When he got into the water, three dolphins, which seemed to want to play **(3)**_____, suddenly appeared near him. Andrew went into the water too and they **(4)**_____ the ball around. The dolphins were swimming after the ball –

(5)_____! **(6)**_____, they took some photos so everyone would believe their story.

Choose **one** of these questions.

Write your answer in about **100 words**.

Question 2

You see this announcement in your school English-language magazine.

> # Articles wanted!
>
> ## Learning a language
>
> What's the best way to learn a language? Is it to have classes with a teacher? Or is going to a country where they speak the language better? Why?
>
> The best articles answering these questions will be published next month.

Write your **article**.

Question 3

Your English teacher has asked you to write a story.

Your story must begin with this sentence.

As they set off on their bikes, they knew they were going to have an exciting day.

Write your **story**.

OVERVIEW
TEST 1: LISTENING

About the paper

There are four parts. You listen to long and short recordings and answer different types of questions. In Parts 1 and 2, you hear short recordings and answer one question about each recording. In Parts 3 and 4, you hear one long recording and answer six questions in each part. You hear each recording twice.

The test lasts approximately 35 minutes. You are given time at the beginning of each part to read the questions. You also have 6 minutes after you have heard all the recordings to transfer your answers to the separate answer sheet.

For Parts 1–4, there is one mark for each correct answer.

How to do the paper

Part 1

In Part 1, there are seven different recordings and a question to answer about each one. In some recordings, you hear one person, for example someone leaving a phone message. In others, you hear two people talking about something in an everyday situation. For each question, there are three pictures (**A**, **B** and **C**). You listen to the question and decide which picture shows the best answer. The questions are mostly about information like times, prices, what people like best or what people decide to do. Listen carefully because the recording mentions the things in all three pictures, but only one picture correctly answers the question.

Part 2

In Part 2, there are six different recordings and they are all conversations between two people. There is one question about each recording, but this time the answers are multiple-choice. You hear a sentence that tells you who is speaking and what they are talking about. Then you have time to read the question and three options (**A**, **B** and **C**). You listen and choose the best option. You need to listen for things like the speakers' attitudes, opinions and feelings. You don't usually hear exactly the same words that you read in the options, so think about the meaning of what the people are saying. Some questions ask about one of the people, but others ask about what the people agree or what they both say. Always listen carefully to what each person says.

Part 3

In Part 3, there is one long recording and there is always just one person talking. For example, you may hear someone giving a presentation or someone making an announcement. You hear a sentence that tells you who is speaking and what they are talking about. You then have time to read a set of notes or sentences from which some of the information is missing. Read this carefully and think about the information you need to fill each of the six gaps. When you listen, follow the information in the task and be ready to write the missing information in the gaps. Write the exact word(s) or number(s) you hear. Always listen carefully because you may hear some of the words that are written in the task or words that mean the same thing. You may also hear more than one word that could fit in a gap so think carefully about the word you need. Sometimes the recording gives the spelling of a word, like somebody's name, for example. Listen to the letters carefully.

Part 4

In Part 4, there is one long recording, which is always an interview. You hear a sentence that tells you who is being interviewed and what the topic is. For example, it could be a school student who has an interesting hobby or a sportsperson or a celebrity. You then have time to read six multiple-choice questions. Each one refers to one of the questions that the interviewer asks in the recording. You listen and choose which option (**A**, **B** or **C**) answers each question. Remember that the questions come in the same order as the information in the recording. Listen carefully and think about the meaning of what the person says. You don't usually hear the same words that are written in the questions or options, but you do hear the person talking about the ideas.

PART 1: TRAINING

Focus on the instructions

1 🔊 Listen to the introduction to the test and answer the questions.

  a How many parts does the whole listening test have?

  b How many times will you listen to each part?

  c What should you do before you listen to each part?

2 Read the instructions for Part 1 and look at the task on pages 30–31.

  a How many questions are there?

  b How many pictures are there for each question?

  c What do you need to do?

Focus on the questions

1 Look at question **1** and the three pictures on page 30.

  a What does each picture show?

  b Think of different ways of saying the first date.

  c What is the key word in the question? Why?

2 🔊 Listen to the recording for question **1**. Answer these questions.

  a Which phrase refers to 'enter the competition'?

  b Which phrase means 'the last date'?

  c What date will the results be announced?

  d What will happen on 27th June?

  e Why is June 24th important?

3 Look at question **2** and pictures **A–C**. Name the different objects in the pictures.

4 In question **3**, what makes each pizza different from the other pizzas?

5 In question **4**, think about how to describe each location.

6 Look at question **5**. What is the same and different in each picture?

7 In question **6** name the different activities.

8 Look at question **7**. Name the different animals on the T-shirts.

9 Look at these extracts from the recordings for questions **1–7**, which focus on the answers to the questions. Complete them using the words and phrases from the box.

> at the latest   by   change my mind
> go with   short   so   too   under that
> went for

  1 You need to upload your photo onto the school website .... June the twenty-fourth ....

  2 In the end, I .... a hand-painted plate.

  3 I was thinking of having the one with red peppers on, but you've made me ....

  4 You'll see a big tree nearby – we'll meet ....

  5 This one's got .... dark hair – nothing special about it really.

  6 The friend I went with really wanted to do that, ... I signed up for that ....

  7 OK, I'll .... your choice then.

10 🔊 Listen and check your answers.

11 Now try the exam task.

Part I

Questions 1 – 7

For each question, choose the correct answer.

---

1 What is the last date for entering the competition?

              A   B   C

2 What did the girl buy on holiday?

        A   B   C

3 Which pizza does the boy decide to have?

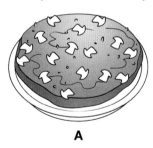 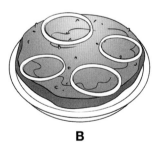 

        A   B   C

4   Where should the students wait?

A   B   C

5   What does the boy's cousin look like?

A   B   C

6   What did the girl do at summer camp?

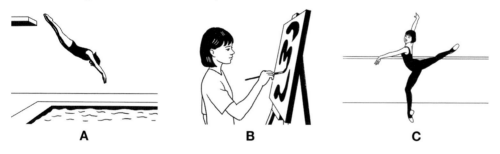

A   B   C

7   Which T-shirt does the boy decide to buy?

A   B   C

PART 2: TRAINING

Focus on the instructions

1 Read the instructions for Part 2 and look at the task on page 33.

   a How many questions are there?

   b How many options do you choose from in each question?

   c What do you need to do?

Focus on the questions

1 🔊 Read question **8** and listen to the recording. Answer these questions.

   a Who says the park should be brought up to date – the girl, the boy, both or neither of them?

   b Who says the park should be kept more tidy – the girl, the boy, both or neither of them?

   c Who says the park should be left as it is – the girl, the boy, both or neither of them?

   d What is the correct answer to question 8?

2 🔊 Now listen to the recording again and answer these questions about it.

   a Do you hear the words 'brought up to date', 'kept more tidy or 'left as it is' in the recording?

   b What do the speakers say that helps you choose the correct answer?

3 Read question **9** and answer these questions.

   a How might the weather spoil the barbecue?

   b How might the food not be well-cooked?

   c How might the place be uncomfortable?

4 🔊 Now listen to the recording again and answer these questions about it.

   a Do the girl and the boy say it rained?

   b Does the boy say his food was good or bad? What about the girl?

   c What does the girl say about where she sat? What does the boy say about the same thing?

   d What is the correct answer to question 9?

5 🔊 Look at question **10**. The correct answer here is **A**. Now listen to the recording for question 10. What does the girl say that tells you she didn't like either the show or the guided tour?

6 🔊 Now look at question **11** and listen to the recording. Answer these questions.

   a Does the boy say his coach is friendly or unfriendly? Does he like his coach anyway? Is he complaining about him?

   b Do you know what the coach makes the boy do? What is it? Does he describe it?

   c Does the boy want the girl to have lessons from his coach? Is he encouraging her?

   d What is the correct answer to question 11?

7 🔊 Look at question **12** and listen to the recording. Answer these questions.

   a Does the girl talk about how long the party went on for?

   b Does she say the organisation was bad?

   c How does the girl say that the party was good value for money?

   d What is the correct answer to question 12?

8 🔊 Finally, look at question **13** and listen to the recording. Answer these questions.

   a Is the girl talking about what she expected to see in the art gallery?

   b Was she more interested in the stories or in the things she saw?

   c Did she enjoy the trip?

   d What is the correct answer for question 13?

Questions 8 – 13

For each question, choose the correct answer.

---

8   You will hear two friends talking about a local park.
     What do they both think?

     A   It should be brought up to date.

     B   It should be kept more tidy.

     C   It should be left as it is.

9   You will hear two friends talking about a barbecue they went to.
     What do they agree about it?

     A   The weather spoilt it.

     B   The food wasn't well cooked.

     C   The place was uncomfortable.

10   You will hear two friends talking about a class trip to the theatre.
     What did the girl like best about it?

     A   meeting the actors

     B   watching the show

     C   having a guided tour

11   You will hear a boy telling a friend about his tennis coach.
     What is he doing?

     A   explaining why he dislikes his coach

     B   describing what his coach makes him do

     C   encouraging her to take lessons with his coach

12   You will hear a girl telling a friend about a family celebration.
     What does she say about it?

     A   It went on too long.

     B   It wasn't well organised.

     C   It was good value for money.

13   You will hear a girl telling a friend about a school trip to an art gallery.
     How did she feel about it?

     A   surprised by things that she saw

     B   interested in stories that she heard

     C   disappointed by what there was to do

Focus on the instructions

1 🔊 Read and listen to the instructions on page 35 and answer the questions.

  a Who will you listen to and what is he doing?

  b What will this person be talking about?

  c What do you need to do?

  d How many words should you write in each gap?

  e Should you write the exact words you hear or think of other words that mean the same?

  f What else might you have to write in a gap apart from words?

2 What should you do before you listen? Choose the correct answer.

  a Read the text and think about possible answers.

  b Read the text and write in some answers.

Focus on the questions

1 Read the task on page 35. Think about the kind of information you will need to write in each gap.

  a In question **14** should you write a noun or an adjective?

  b In question **15** do you have to write a person or an object?

  c What might go in the gap in question **16**?

  d How could you complete question **17**?

  e In question **18** should you write a place or a person?

  f What might go in the gap in question **19**?

2 Look at the exam task on page 35. Which word from the box below should go in each gap?

> brown   drawing   film   geography
> iceberg   pencil case   photographs
> subjects   striped   uncle   waterfall

3 🔊 Listen and check your answers.

Focus on the language

1 Choose the correct words to complete these extracts from the recording for the task on page 35.

  a As a kid, she was really keen *on / with* butterflies.

  b I never thought she'd win, *but / and* she did.

  c As part of her course, she has to *pass / spend* a month doing research in another country.

  d Maybe that's why nobody *never / ever* sees one!

  e Then, on the last day, she was sitting next to a waterfall, *when / because* a butterfly settled on her rucksack.

  f Megan said it was, like, *a / an* awesome experience.

2 🔊 Listen and check your answers.

Part 3

Questions 14 – 19

For each question, write the correct answer in the gap. Write **one** or **two words** or a **number** or a **date** or a **time**.

You will hear a boy giving a class presentation about his older sister, Megan, who has a butterfly named after her.

Megan and the butterfly

As a child, Megan's favourite **(14)**.................... had a picture of a butterfly on it.

Megan's **(15)**.................... persuaded her to enter a competition to name a butterfly.

Megan is now studying **(16)**.................... at university.

Megan's butterfly is mostly **(17)**.................... in colour.

In Brazil, Megan eventually saw her butterfly near to a **(18)**.................... .

To see a **(19)**.................... of Megan's butterfly, go to the university website.

PART 4: TRAINING

Focus on the instructions

1 🔊 Read and listen to the instructions on page 37.

 a How many questions are there?

 b How many options do you choose from?

 c What are you told about the situation?

 d What do you need to do **before** you listen?

Focus on the questions

1 Look at questions **20–25** from the task on page 37. Underline the most important word(s) in each question.

2 🔊 Look at question **20** and listen to the recording.

 a Does Selina say she'd always wanted to start a club, or just that she'd played chess since she was a child?

 b Did her school want to have a club before she mentioned it?

3 Now look at question **21** and answer these questions.

 a Does Selina say it's a good idea to buy equipment from different places, or the same place?

 b Why does Selina say there might be a problem with the cheapest equipment?

4 In the recording for question **22** ...

 a Does Selina say it's possible for players to always compete against the same people?

 b Does Selina say the best players teach the new members?

5 Look at question **23** and listen to the recording. Answer these questions.

 a Did Selina lose any equipment?

 b Does the club have enough space for all the players?

6 In the recording for question **24** ...

 a Does Selina say that students can play chess online?

 b Does Selina think that chess helps students with their schoolwork directly?

7 Now look at the last question, **25**, and listen to the recording. Answer these questions.

 a How good does Selina think her chess club members are?

 b Does she recommend all students play chess?

Focus on the language

1 These extracts show where the answers to questions **20–25** can be found. Complete them using the words from the box.

> against   at once   different   jokes
> ought to   whatever   work things out

 1 When I heard he'd joined a chess club there, I thought we .... have one at my school, too.

 2 But buy them all .... , from the same place, and you'll get a pretty good discount.

 3 It's also important that anyone coming for the first time feels welcome, ... their level.

 4 It only ever happened once when one boy kept telling silly .... and nobody could concentrate.

 5 Playing a game of chess teaches you how to .... in your head.

 6 It'd be good to play .... clubs from other schools sometimes – it's always interesting to meet players who approach the game in .... ways.

2 🔊 Listen and check your answers.

Part 4

You will hear an interview with a girl called Selina Stead who runs a chess club at her school.

For each question, choose the correct answer.

20   Why did Selina decide to start a school chess club?

   A   A family member gave her the idea.

   B   It was something she'd always wanted to do.

   C   Her school was looking for somebody to do it.

21   Selina says that when buying chess equipment, it's best to

   A   buy it from different places.

   B   get a large amount at the same time.

   C   go to the company with lowest prices.

22   At club sessions, Selina likes to make sure

   A   members can always choose who they play against.

   B   new members can learn from the best players.

   C   all members get an enjoyable game.

23   Selina had to ask for the help of a teacher when

   A   some of the club's property went missing.

   B   one of the club's members behaved badly.

   C   the club needed space for extra sessions.

24   Selina says that playing chess can help students to

   A   spend less time online.

   B   concentrate better in class.

   C   think more clearly.

25   In future, Selina would like the chess club to

   A   play chess against other schools.

   B   enter chess competitions at national level.

   C   get everyone in the school interested in chess.

OVERVIEW
TEST 1: SPEAKING

About the paper

The Speaking Test lasts approximately 12 minutes and there are four parts. Parts 1 and 2 take 2–3 minutes each. Parts 3 and 4 take 6 minutes in total. You take the test with a partner. There are two examiners. One examiner acts as interlocutor and speaks to you, the other just listens. In some parts you talk to the examiner, and in other parts you talk to each other.

The examiner who listens marks you all through the test, and gives marks for the grammar and vocabulary you use, how you organise what you say, your pronunciation, and the way you interact with your partner and with the examiner. The interlocutor also gives you a global mark. The speaking mark is 25 percent of your total score for the whole test.

How to do the paper

Part 1

In Part 1, the examiner asks each of you questions about yourselves. You speak to the examiner in this part, and not to each other. The first few questions are simple ones, for example: your name, how old you are, where you live and who you live with. You just give short simple answers to these questions.

After this, the examiner asks you each one or two more personal questions, for example about your likes and dislikes or your daily routines. You should give longer answers to these questions. Try to think of something interesting to say and keep talking until the examiner says 'Thank you.'

Part 2

In Part 2, you also speak to the examiner, but there are no questions to answer. In this part, the examiner gives you each a photograph of an everyday situation to talk about. Your photo will show people at home or at school, or maybe doing an outdoor activity. You should say what you can see in the photograph and describe all the details; for example, where it is, what the people are doing, what they're wearing, how they're feeling and so on. Keep talking until the examiner says 'Thank you.' You should try to organise what you say; for example, begin by describing the people and what they're doing before moving on to talk about the things in the background.

Part 3

In Part 3, the examiner describes a situation to you, and gives you a picture with some ideas to discuss with your partner. The examiner doesn't ask you questions; instead, you have to speak to your partner. Listen carefully to the situation that the examiner describes to you, and the question you need to discuss. Look at the ideas around the main picture. You and your partner should exchange your suggestions and opinions about these. Try to talk about all the ideas before you come to a decision, and say why each one is good or bad. You have to keep talking for 2–3 minutes until the examiner says 'Thank you'. Remember to ask your partner questions, and respond to your partner's ideas, because you get marks for interacting well with each other.

Part 4

In Part 4, the examiner asks you and your partner some more questions that are connected to the topic of your discussion in Part 3. You should give your own opinion and say why you think that. Listen to your partner's questions and their answers because you may be asked if you agree, or to give your own opinion about the same question.

See **SPEAKING BANK** for useful language and practice
See **GRAMMAR BANK** for reference and practice

OVERVIEW SPEAKING

PARTS 1–4: TRAINING

Focus on Part 1

1 Answer these questions from Phase 1.

  a What's your name?

  b How old are you?

  c Where do you live?

  d Who do you live with?

2 Match the examiner's questions **1–4** from Phase 2 with the student's answers **A–D**.

  1 Do you do any sport at school?

  2 Tell us about a teacher you like.

  3 What do you enjoy doing in your free time?

  4 Where would you like to go on your next holiday?

  A My maths teacher is really nice and very patient. She explains everything very well and helps us if we don't understand.

  B I play football twice a week, but actually I'm not very good at it. I quite enjoy trying, though, and our coach is really nice!

  C I'm keen on the beach but I also like cities, so I'd love to visit Barcelona because that has both.

  D I'm really into sport and so I try to play tennis every week when I have free time. I have a lot of homework to do, though!

Focus on Part 2

1 Look at photograph **1A** on page 192. Read a student's description of the photograph. Choose the correct word to fill each gap.

> I can see five friends who are studying together **(1)** *around / near* a table. I think they're in a library **(2)** *while / because* I can see lots of books on shelves behind them. They're not wearing school uniform, though I **(3)** *suppose / say* they're in school. There are books on the table. The girl **(4)** *on / in* the left has long blond hair, and she's wearing headphones and a pink shirt. The boy next to her is **(5)** *carrying / wearing* a checked shirt and white T-shirt and they're studying a book together. They're both concentrating hard. The girl in the **(6)** *middle / between* has long brown hair and she's wearing a blue T-shirt. She's holding a pen **(7)** *but / and* making notes in her notebook. She's sitting next to a girl **(8)** *who / that* is wearing a grey jumper, and next to her is a boy who's standing up. **(9)** *These / They* three friends on the right are also studying a book. **(10)** *It / There* is also a tablet on the table in front of them.

Focus on Part 3

1 Look at the task on page 200. Match the expressions (**1–4**) which a student used to talk about it with the functions (**A–D**).

  1 I think the boy should go fishing.

  2 Do you really think that's a good idea?

  3 What do you think about the idea of rock-climbing?

  4 You're right about that.

  A Agreeing

  B Disagreeing

  C Asking for your partner's opinion

  D Giving your own opinion

Focus on Part 4

1 Read the examiner's questions and the two students' answers for each one. Which is the best answer in each case, **A** or **B**? Why?

  Int: Do you enjoy taking part in competitions?

  A: Not really – I never seem to win anything! So I don't enjoy them much. My sister loves them though.

  B: No – not at all! I hate them.

  Int: Do you usually prefer to do indoor or outdoor activities in your free time?

  A: I definitely prefer being outdoors because I spend a lot of time in school during the week. I often go jogging with my friends, and I love horse riding.

  B: You do activities like football, rugby and cycling outside but basketball, badminton and judo inside.

Part 1 (2–3 minutes)

Phase 1

In Phase 1 of Part 1, the examiner asks you and your partner questions about yourselves. This is what the examiner says.

Good morning/afternoon/evening.

Can I have your mark sheets, please?

I'm … and this is …

- What's your name?
- How old are you?
- Where do you live?
- Who do you live with?

> **Back-up prompts**
> These are some further questions the examiner may ask:
> *Do you live in (name of town, city or region)?*
> *Do you live with your family?*

Phase 2

In Phase 2 of Part 1, the examiner asks you each a few questions about your likes and dislikes and daily routines. For example, the examiner may ask you questions like:

- What's your favourite subject at school? (Why?)
- How do you travel to school every day?
- Tell us about your best friend.
- Do you watch a lot of television programmes? (Why?/Why not?)
- Do you get a lot of homework?
- What part of the day do you like best? (Why?)
- Do you enjoy going to the cinema? (Why?/Why not?)
- Do you prefer winter or summer holidays? (Why?)

> **Back-up prompts**
> These are some further questions the examiner may ask:
> *Did you do anything special yesterday? What was it?*
> *Who is in your family?*
> *Where do you usually go on holiday?*
> *Did you have a party on your last birthday?*

Part 2 (2–3 minutes)

In Part 2, the examiner asks you each to describe a photograph. This is what the examiner says.

1A Studying

Now, I'd like each of you to talk on your own about something.

I'm going to give each of you a photograph and I'd like you to talk about it.

A, here is your photograph. It shows **friends studying together**.

[*Turn to photograph 1A on page 192.*]

B, you just listen.

A, please tell us what you can see in the photograph.

 about 1 minute

Thank you.

1B At a picnic

B, here is your photograph. It shows **friends having a picnic**.

[*Turn to photograph 1B on page 196.*]

A, you just listen.

B, please tell us what you can see in the photograph.

> **Back-up prompts**
> These are some things the examiner may say to help you answer:
> *Talk about the people.*
> *Talk about the place.*
> *Talk about other things in the photograph.*

about 1 minute

Thank you.

Part 3 (2–3 minutes)

In Part 3, the examiner asks you to do a task together. This is what the examiner says.

Now, in this part of the test, you're going to talk about something together for about two minutes. I'm going to describe a situation to you.

[*Turn to the task on page 200.*]

A boy has just moved to a different town. He wants to start a new hobby so that he can make more friends. He likes being outside, but he doesn't have much spare time to learn to do difficult things.

Here are some hobbies he could do.

Talk together about the different hobbies he could do, and say which would be best.

All right? Now, talk together.

 2–3 minutes

Thank you.

Part 4 (2–3 minutes)

In Part 4, the examiner asks you each a few questions about the topic in general. For example, the examiner may ask you questions like:

- What's your favourite hobby? (Why?)
- Would you like to start a new hobby soon? (Why?/Why not?)
- Do you usually prefer to do indoor or outdoor activities in your free time? (Why?)
- Do you enjoy taking part in competitions? (Why?/Why not?)
- Do you think it's better to have lots of different hobbies or be very good at just one? (Why?)

> **Back-up prompts**
> The examiner may ask you to respond to your partner's answers, with questions like:
> *How/What about you?*
> *Do you agree?*
> *What do you think?*

 2–3 minutes

Thank you. That is the end of the test.

Part 1

Questions 1 – 5

For each question, choose the correct answer.

1

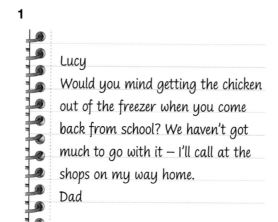

Lucy

Would you mind getting the chicken out of the freezer when you come back from school? We haven't got much to go with it – I'll call at the shops on my way home.

Dad

A Lucy's dad would like Lucy to make the dinner tonight.

B Lucy should buy something to eat with the chicken after school.

C Lucy needs to take something from the freezer when she gets home.

TIP STRIP

Question 1: In the message to Lucy, who is going to the shops? And what does Lucy have to do with the chicken?

Question 2: What have some students worn in sports lessons recently? Is this the correct kit?

Question 3: Has someone already cancelled the game?

2

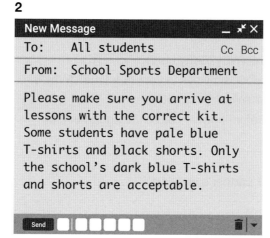

New Message

To: All students

From: School Sports Department

Please make sure you arrive at lessons with the correct kit. Some students have pale blue T-shirts and black shorts. Only the school's dark blue T-shirts and shorts are acceptable.

A The school has recently changed the colour of its sports kit.

B Several students have worn the wrong kit in sports lessons.

C The sports department doesn't want students to wear dark blue kit.

3

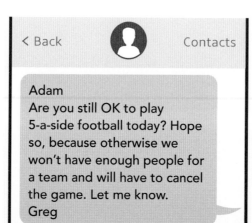

< Back   Contacts

Adam
Are you still OK to play 5-a-side football today? Hope so, because otherwise we won't have enough people for a team and will have to cancel the game. Let me know.
Greg

A Greg is checking that Adam can keep an arrangement they made previously.

B A player in Greg's football team can't play so he's asking Adam instead.

C Greg wants to ask Adam why the football game they'd arranged is cancelled.

4

A coat has gone missing
from the changing room.

If found, please hand it in
to the school secretary.

A See the school secretary if you left a coat in the changing room.

B Someone has lost a coat that they left in the changing room.

C It's not possible to leave coats in the changing room at the moment.

TIP STRIP

Question 4: If a coat has gone missing, does that mean that someone has lost it?

Question 5: What does the word 'free' mean in the notice?

5

Library users are advised
that computers must be
booked with a staff
member, even when
machines appear to be free.

A You do not have to pay for using any of the library's computers.

B See a member of staff if you need advice about using the computers.

C Anyone wanting to use a computer should see a member of staff first.

Part 2

Questions 6 – 10

For each question, choose the correct answer.

The young people below all want to find a campsite to go to with their families.

On the opposite page there are eight descriptions of campsites.

Decide which campsite would be most suitable for the people below.

6  Amjad wants to go to a campsite which has a restaurant and that has a beach nearby. He'd like there to be organised day trips to places of interest.

7  Jing would like to find a campsite in the mountains which has a swimming pool. She would like to learn how to do some water sports while she's there.

8  Pascal would like to hire bikes at the campsite he goes to. He wants a campsite that's near a big city and that has a disco every week.

9  Karolina wants a campsite with entertainment for her six-year-old brother so she doesn't have to look after him so much. Her family are travelling by plane and like having tents that are already set up.

10  Michael would like to go to a campsite that's close to a river and that he can travel to by train. He'd like there to be different activities for teenagers available every day.

Campsites

A   The Ridge

This small campsite located in beautiful mountains is great for families. It's only a 10-minute taxi ride from the nearest airport and you won't even need to pack or put up a tent, as these are all provided for you. There are activities and shows for under-10s every day, and for teenagers, too, on weekdays.

B   Camping Deluxe

Just 200 m from the sea, Camping Deluxe is a great place for those who love water sports or just relaxing on the beach. There's bike hire at the campsite that's reasonably priced. It's only a short bus ride from the town of Dannbury and its railway station.

C   The Pines

Situated by a lake among beautiful mountains, The Pines offers activities for all ages, including swimming, sailing and windsurfing from the campsite's beach. The owners arrange visits to several cities and to many historical buildings in the area. It has one of the best places to eat in the region.

D   Country Camping

Perfect for families, Country Camping organises things to do for all age groups daily. Perhaps you'll love the weekly disco, or maybe sailing or swimming in the river nearby is more your thing? It's just 1 km to the nearest railway station and only 500 m to the shops and restaurants of the local village.

E   Freetime Camping

Definitely a campsite for the more active family, Freetime Camping has three large pools to choose from, as well as mountain bike hire and day trips to the seaside or to the famous national railway museum. There's something for everyone, whether you're six years old or sixty.

F   Camp Best

Bring your own tent or use one of the many that Camp Best provides for guests – it's up to you! From music and dancing every Saturday to cheap cycle hire, Camp Best has it all. Only 5 km outside the capital, with its restaurants, shops, train stations and airport, it's a great place to be.

G   The Granary

The Granary has one of the best waterslides and pools in the country, as well as a beach only a five-minute walk away. There are daily organised activities for everyone, from the youngest children to adults. The weekly disco is incredibly popular, especially among teenage campers.

H   Habitat Camping

A great place for lovers of the outdoors – guests can take classes in windsurfing and sailing, or rent a bike and spend the day riding on one of the many mountain paths in the local area. They can cool off afterwards in the pool and then eat at the site's convenient restaurant.

Questions 11 – 15

For each question, choose the correct answer.

My flying experience

Twelve-year-old Jessica Gilligan describes how she flew a small plane

I'd never thought of flying as something I would ever actually want to do in my free time until my family bought me what's called a 'flying experience day' as a birthday present. Don't get me wrong, I wasn't like some of my friends, who would start shaking with fear at the thought of going in a plane of any size. I'd actually always looked forward to flying off somewhere on holiday, especially that feeling you get when the plane's just taking off. But flying a plane was something other people did, not me.

I started researching the experience day online straight away. The little aircraft I was going to fly in could only go up to 3000 metres, which is quite low when you realise big jets fly closer to 10000 metres. I found out there was a half-hour talk from the instructor about safety and the controls. This seemed more than enough to me, as I was only going to be in the air for about the same amount of time, which I couldn't quite believe. My parents were amazed that something like that was available for twelve-year-olds, but I'm very pleased it was.

On the day, I was quite nervous but Sheena, my instructor, was very calm, which helped a lot. She took the controls as we took off, of course. It appeared to take ages to get high up, but it was only actually a minute or two, and then I took the controls. I was so excited, I wasn't really listening to what Sheena was saying. I was hoping to see my house but it was hard to work out where everything was from the air. Even though we were flying at 280 kilometres per hour, you could hardly tell we were moving when you looked down.

I'm now so into flying that I'm considering it as a career. I'll need to become qualified, of course, and I'm happy to save up for more classes to do this. It was such fun that I'd love to do it every day and get paid for it, too. The company that organises experience days keeps sending emails about train driving and other things, but I only want more of one particular kind of experience now!

11 How did Jessica feel about flying before she did the flying experience day?

    A scared of flying in a small plane

    B confident that she would be good at it

    C uninterested in taking it up as a hobby

    D curious about what it would feel like

12 What surprised Jessica as she was researching the flying experience day?

    A the low age limit

    B the lack of training

    C the height the plane would reach

    D the length of the flight

13 What does Jessica say about being in the air?

    A the plane appeared to travel very slowly

    B seeing where she lives was incredible

    C it was too noisy to hear the instructor

    D they seemed to climb very quickly

14 What does Jessica hope to do in the future?

    A have more flying lessons just for fun

    B attempt to get a pilot's licence

    C try different 'experience days'

    D learn how to handle other vehicles

15 What would Jessica's mum say about her?

    A I can't believe Jessica's gone so quickly from someone who got quite bored during flights to someone who goes flying every weekend.

    B We only bought her that present after she'd found out that the experience day was open to twelve-year-olds.

    C Jessica will want money for her birthday from now on but at least she'll be using it for something she loves.

    D Jessica was so relaxed when we arrived for the flying experience day, so I was surprised she got so anxious after taking off.

TIP STRIP

Question 11: Was Jessica scared of flying? Did she show any interest in learning how to fly?

Question 12: Was Jessica surprised by how little training there was? Who was surprised about the age limit?

Question 13: Does Jessica say she could see her house? What does she say about how fast the plane was flying?

Question 14: What does Jessica say about other experience days? Does she say she wants to go on another which involves trains?

Question 15: Does Jessica say she used to get bored during flights? What does Jessica say about money and flying lessons in the future?

Part 4

Questions 16 – 20

Five sentences have been removed from the text below.

For each question, choose the correct answer.

There are three extra sentences which you do not need to use.

The Tomatina Festival

The Tomatina Festival takes place every August in the small Spanish town of Buñol. It has been described as the world's biggest food fight, as the most famous part of the celebrations involve 20 000 people throwing tomatoes at each other!

No one is totally sure how the festival began, but it seems to have started in the 1940s. One story tells how some teenage friends started throwing old tomatoes at one another for fun. **16** [   ] Another describes how the crowd at a more traditional festival was so bored by the entertainment, they started throwing tomatoes at the entertainers and then at each other! Whatever the truth is, the event was repeated the following year and its popularity has grown ever since.

On the day of the festival, several large lorries, loaded with over 100 000 kg of soft, ripe tomatoes, appear in the town square. Everyone helps themselves or is given lots of the tomatoes, and once a special signal is given, the tomato fight begins. **17** [   ] After another signal, everyone stops throwing the fruit and the clean up begins.

At one time, over 40 000 people attended the festival (Buñol's population is only around 9000!) but this was felt to be too many, so the organisers decided to introduce a limit. This was set at a maximum of 20 000 people per year. **18** [   ] Without this, you will not be allowed to take part.

The organisers give lots of advice to anyone who is involved in the festival's tomato fight. They suggest that festival-goers only wear things that they are happy to throw away afterwards. **19** [   ] Other advice is to avoid bringing a camera, as unless it is a special waterproof one, it is almost certain to get damaged. People are also asked to make sure that the tomatoes are as soft as possible before they throw them. **20** [   ] But above all, the organisers just want visitors to the Tomatina festival to have fun!

A   They will certainly never be the same colour again!

B   That is why they also began throwing the fruit at everyone.

C   It generally lasts for about one hour.

D   This will hopefully stop them from injuring anyone.

E   There were as many as 50 000 visitors that year.

F   This seemed so enjoyable that other people joined in.

G   For this reason, the organisers stopped people bringing glass bottles.

H   So these days, you actually need a ticket to attend.

Part 5

Questions 21 – 26

For each question, choose the correct answer.

The history of surfing

Surfing is one of the oldest sports on the planet. No one really knows **(21)**................ when it first started but it is **(22)**................ that people have used wooden boards to ride waves for about three thousand years. The first surfers were probably fishermen from islands in the Pacific Ocean, who found that bringing the fish they had **(23)**................ to shore was much easier if they rode waves onto the beach in their small boats. Over time, this developed from part of the working day into a **(24)**................ activity.

The first **(25)**................ records of surfing appeared in the late eighteenth century. English explorer Captain James Cook wrote in his diary about seeing locals riding the waves for **(26)**................ on a Pacific island called Tahiti.

In the early twentieth century, surfing spread to the US state of California and Australia. It's now popular all around the world.

21	A	certainly	B	correctly	C	exactly	D	totally
22	A	thought	B	supposed	C	intended	D	expected
23	A	gained	B	kept	C	held	D	caught
24	A	rest	B	leisure	C	relaxation	D	entertainment
25	A	ancient	B	historical	C	antique	D	old
26	A	pleasure	B	happiness	C	wish	D	choice

Part 6

Questions 27 – 32

For each question, write the correct answer.

Write **one** word for each gap.

My drama club

In my blog today, I'm going to tell you about the drama club I go to. I first found out

(27)............... it from a friend of mine. He recommended it to me around six months

(28)............... and I joined immediately.

I really love going because I think the teacher there is the **(29)**............... amazing

teacher ever! The activities we do in classes are really interesting and I'm getting so

much better **(30)**............... acting, thanks to all the things we do there. **(31)**...............

I got the chance, I'd really like to become a professional actor in the future, but I

know **(32)**............... difficult it can be to become successful. So many people want

to become actors but very few actually achieve their dream.

TIP STRIP

Question 27: Which word comes after the phrasal verb 'find out'?

Question 28: Which word can we put here that tells us this time is in the past?

Question 29: Which word goes here to make a superlative?

Question 30: Which short word do you need in the phrase 'good __ something'?

Question 31: Which word do we often use in conditional sentences like this one?

Question 32: Which question word do you need to use here?

Part 1

You **must** answer this question.

Write your answer in about **100 words**.

Question 1

Read this email from your English-speaking friend Sam and the notes you have made.

New Message
From: Sam
Subject: Learning the guitar
Hi I know you play the guitar really well. Guess what! I've just started learning, too. ◄ ········· *Fantastic!* I was wondering if you'd be able to give me some advice. How often do you practise, and for how long? ◄ ········· *Tell Sam* Should I buy a guitar straight away or just use the one the school has lent me for now? ◄ ········· *Say which is better* Would you be able to teach me how to play some simple songs? ◄ ········· *Yes, but …* See you soon Sam

Write your **email** to Sam using **all the notes**.

Part 2

Choose **one** of these questions.

Write your answer in about **100 words**.

Question 2
You see this announcement in your school English-language magazine.

> **Articles wanted!**
> **The time you spend online**
> How much time do you spend online each day on computers and mobile phones?
> Do you think parents should limit how long their children can spend online each day?
> What are the benefits of spending less time online?
> The best articles answering these questions will be published next month.

Write your **article**.

Question 3
Your English teacher has asked you to write a story.
Your story must begin with this sentence.
Anna had just got out of bed when the phone suddenly started ringing.
Write your **story**.

TIP STRIP

Part 1

Question 1:

Remember that the test is about English, not your knowledge of music! So there are no right or wrong answers.

How often do you think good musicians practice, and for how long each day? You need to say a length of time and how often.

Should someone buy an expensive musical instrument if they've only just started playing? What are the reasons for your opinion?

What problems could there be teaching a beginner how to play the guitar?

Part 2

Question 2:

How would you feel if your parents limited the amount of time you could spend online each day? Are there any benefits to spending less time online?

Question 3:

Who do you think was calling? What did they want? What happened next? How might the story end?

Questions 1 – 7

For each question, choose the correct answer.

1   How will the girl get to school on Monday?

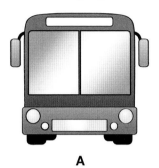
A

B

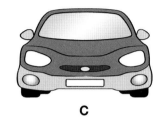
C

2   What did the boy do at the adventure camp?

A

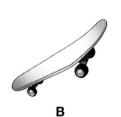
B

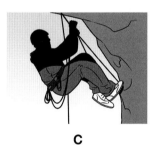
C

3   Where is the girl's bag?

A

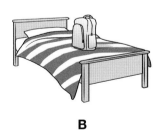
B

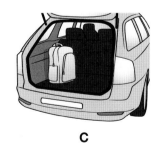
C

TIP STRIP

Question 1: Keep listening. The girl decides what to do at the end.

Question 2: Listen for what the boy 'really wanted' to do. Was he able to do that in the end?

Question 3: Be careful, the table, the bed and the car are all mentioned. We hear where the bag isn't – so where must it be?

4 What time does the television programme start?

A

B

C

TIP STRIP

Question 4: Listen for what the girl says about the time of the programme.

Question 5: Listen for the word 'tomorrow' – the answer comes after this.

Question 6: Which scarf does the boy like? Is that the one the girl chooses?

Question 7: Listen carefully. The teacher talks about all three things. But what should the students 'bring to class'?

5 What will the weather be like tomorrow?

A

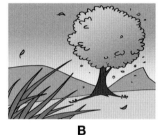

B

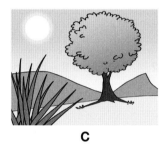

C

6 Which scarf does the girl buy?

A

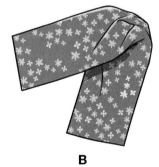

B

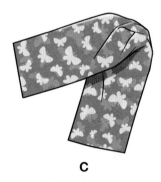

C

7 What should the students bring to class next week?

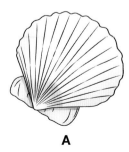

A

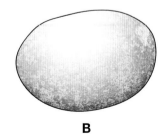

B

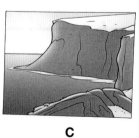

C

Questions 8 – 13

For each question, choose the correct answer.

8   You will hear a girl telling a friend about her new mobile phone.
    What is she pleased about?

   A   how much it cost

   B   the size of the screen

   C   the things she can download on it

9   You will hear a boy telling a friend about learning to play the piano.
    How does he feel about it?

   A   he'd like to improve more quickly

   B   he prefers it to his previous instrument

   C   he enjoys the kind of music he usually plays

10   You will hear a girl telling a friend about a climbing course.
     What did she like best about it?

   A   the people she met

   B   the skills she learnt

   C   the confidence she gained

11   You will hear a boy telling a friend about a photography competition.
     What is he complaining about?

   A   the quality of the prizes

   B   the way it was organised

   C   the opinion of the judges

12   You will hear two friends talking about some homework.
     What do they agree about it?

   A   The topic is interesting.

   B   They need to do it quickly.

   C   It's a hard thing to write about.

13   You will hear a boy telling a friend about a book he's read.
     What did he think of it?

   A   It was better than the film.

   B   The characters were realistic.

   C   The story was rather confusing.

TIP STRIP

Question 8: What's another way of saying 'pleased'? Listen for words that tell you about *the cost*, *the size* and *downloads*.

Question 9: Listen for how learning the piano is different to learning the guitar.

Question 10: Listen for a phrase that matches the idea 'liked best'.

Question 11: You don't hear the words *prizes*, *organised* or *judges*, but you do hear the boy talking about these things.

Question 12: You're listening for something they have the same opinion about.

Question 13: You don't hear the words *film*, *characters* or *story*, so listen for words and phrases that mean the same thing.

Part 3

Questions 14 – 19

For each question, write the correct answer in the gap. Write **one** or **two words** or a **number** or a **date** or a **time**.

You will hear a girl called Susie talking about a llama trekking trip she went on.

Llama Trekking Trip

The llama trek starts at a **(14)**...................

There were a total of **(15)**................... people taking part in Susie's trek.

Susie says that llama trekking is a very **(16)**................... activity.

Walking near a **(17)**................... was the most enjoyable part of Susie's trek.

Susie bought **(18)**................... as a souvenir.

The name of the company that organises the treks is **(19)**................... llamas.

TIP STRIP

Question 14: Listen for where you go if you want to do a llama trek.

Question 15: Be careful, four numbers are mentioned. You're listening for how many people did the trek.

Question 16: Listen for the word that Susie uses to describe the activity.

Question 17: Listen for a phrase that means 'most enjoyable'.

Question 18: Be careful – three souvenirs are mentioned. What did Susie buy for herself?

Question 19: You're listening for the name. It is spelled for you on the recording.

Part 4

Questions 20 – 25

For each question, choose the correct answer.

You will hear an interview with a boy called Joe Stone, who's talking about a drama group he belongs to.

20 Joe decided to join the drama group because

  A it seemed to suit his character.

  B some people he knew were in it.

  C he thought he had a talent for acting.

21 Joe explains that the drama group

  A often puts performances online.

  B does just one large annual show.

  C has members of all different ages.

22 What does Joe say about preparing for his first show?

  A There was more to do than he expected.

  B He enjoyed the physical side of it.

  C It was fun working with others.

23 When asked if the drama club affects his schoolwork, Joe

  A admits that his teachers get worried.

  B describes how his parents support him.

  C explains that it's just like any other hobby.

24 What problem did Joe have with some equipment during one show?

  A It failed to arrive on time.

  B He didn't know how it worked.

  C There was a fault he had to mend.

25 What does Joe like most about the drama group?

  A the way that it makes him feel

  B the range of parts he gets to play

  C the chance of a career it offers him

TIP STRIP

Question 20: You're listening for why Joe decided to join the group.

Question 21: Be careful. You hear the words *online*, *show* and *age*.

Question 22: Listen for what surprised Joe about getting ready for the show.

Question 23: Think about what the three verbs *admits*, *describes* and *explains* mean.

Question 24: Listen for the word 'fortunately' – the answer comes soon afterwards.

Question 25: Joe talks about job interviews. What is that an example of?

Part 1 (2–3 minutes)

Phase 1

- • What's your name?
- • How old are you?
- • Where do you live?
- • Who do you live with?

TIP STRIP

Part 1 Phase 1

Give short answers to the examiner's questions.

Don't talk to your partner in this part.

The questions are always about you and you can practise the answers before the test.

Tell the examiner something interesting about your home or family, but don't say too much.

Answer the question you are asked – don't start talking about other things.

Phase 2

- • What did you do last weekend?
- • How much homework do you do every day?
- • Do you listen to music very often? (Why?/Why not?)
- • Where do you like to meet your friends? (Why?)
- • Which languages do you like studying? (Why?)
- • Do you enjoy shopping? (Why?/Why not?)
- • What's your favourite food? (Why?)
- • Do you like winter or summer best? (Why?)

Part 2 (2–3 minutes)

2A Waiting for a train

Now I'd like each of you to talk on your own about something.
I'm going to give each of you a photograph and I'd like you to talk about it.

A, here is your photograph. It shows **people waiting for a train**.

[*Turn to photograph 2A on page 192.*]

B, you just listen.

A, please tell us what you can see in the photograph.

🕐 about 1 minute

Thank you.

2B Playing basketball

B, here is your photograph. It shows **people playing basketball**.

[*Turn to photograph 2B on page 196.*]

A, you just listen.

B, please tell us what you can see in the photograph.

🕐 about 1 minute

Thank you.

TIP STRIP

Part 1 Phase 2

Give longer answers to these questions. Don't just say 'yes' or 'no'.

Don't talk to your partner in this part; the examiner asks you different questions in turn.

Be ready to talk about things like your studies, what you like to do in your free time, etc.

Try to give interesting details, reasons and examples in your answer.

Part 2

Begin your description by talking about the situation, where the people are and what they're doing.

Describe the people: how old they are; what their relationship is; what they're wearing; how they're feeling, etc.

Give reasons for your ideas, for example, *I think she's feeling happy because ... .*

Talk about everything you can see in the photograph but don't worry if you don't know a particular word.

Part 3 (2–3 minutes)

Now, in this part of the test you're going to talk about something together for about two minutes. I'm going to describe a situation to you.

[*Turn to the task on page 201.*]

A girl is moving to a new apartment with her family. Her friends want to buy her a present for her room in the new apartment.

Here are some things her friends could buy.

Talk together about the different things the friends could buy for the girl's room and say which would be best.

All right? Now talk together.

 2–3 minutes

Thank you.

TIP STRIP

Part 3

Talk to your partner, not the examiner.

Ask your partner questions, for example, *What do you think of this one?*

You can also ask your partner to comment on your ideas: *I think this one is a good idea. What do you think?*

Talk about all the things in the task – you could start with things that aren't such a good idea.

Don't decide on the best thing too quickly – you have to talk for about two minutes!

Give reasons for your opinions, for example, *I don't think this is a good idea because ... .*

Remember, you don't have to agree with your partner and there's no right answer.

Part 4 (2–3 minutes)

- Have you ever bought a present for a friend's room? (What was it?)
- Do you like the house or apartment you live in? (Why?/Why not?)
- What do you like best about the town or city where you live now? (Why?)
- Is it important to live near school friends? (Why?/Why not?)
- Where would you like to live in the future? (Why?)

 2–3 minutes

Thank you. That is the end of the test.

TIP STRIP

Part 4

The questions in Part 4 are on a similar topic to Part 3, but they're not about that exact situation. These questions ask what you think about life in general.

Give longer answers to these questions and give reasons for your answers.

Give examples and explanations to support your ideas.

Listen to what your partner says because the examiner may ask *Do you agree?*, *How/What about you?* or *What do you think?* after he/she has finished speaking. Then you can agree or disagree with what your partner has said.

Part 1

Questions 1 – 5

For each question, choose the correct answer.

1

Extra help with maths

We're looking for students who are willing to spend one lunchtime a week providing extra maths sessions to students needing help with this subject. Interested?

Please see the school secretary.

See the school secretary if

A   you think you need extra help with maths.

B   you want to teach maths to other students.

C   you'd like to join a lunchtime maths club.

2

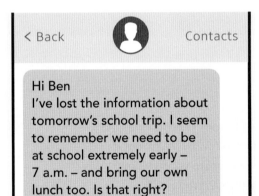

< Back   Contacts

Hi Ben
I've lost the information about tomorrow's school trip. I seem to remember we need to be at school extremely early – 7 a.m. – and bring our own lunch too. Is that right?
Tom

Tom is texting Ben to

A   give him some information about a school trip.

B   complain about the arrangements for a school trip.

C   check the details of a school trip with him.

3

Cycling is permitted only in certain areas of the park. Paths not clearly marked with signs are for pedestrians only.

A   Cyclists should check for notices showing where they can and can't cycle.

B   Cyclists should only use paths which don't have signs on them.

C   Cyclists should get off and walk through all parts of the park.

4

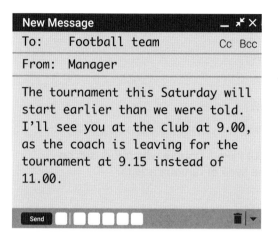

New Message _ ⤢ ✕

To: Football team   Cc Bcc

From: Manager

The tournament this Saturday will start earlier than we were told. I'll see you at the club at 9.00, as the coach is leaving for the tournament at 9.15 instead of 11.00.

Send ☐☐☐☐☐☐   🗑 ▼

How have the arrangements for the football tournament changed?

A   The manager will now meet the players at the tournament at 11.00.

B   The coach will now leave at 9.15 and arrive at the tournament at 11.00.

C   The players and manager will now set off for the tournament together at 9.15.

5

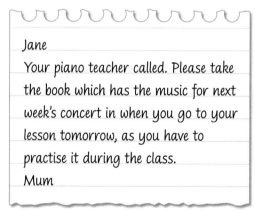

Jane

Your piano teacher called. Please take the book which has the music for next week's concert in when you go to your lesson tomorrow, as you have to practise it during the class.

Mum

A   Jane needs to take her music book when she goes to the concert next week.

B   Jane's appearing in a concert soon and must practise the music for it tomorrow.

C   Jane's piano teacher wants her to practise the concert music before her lesson.

Part 2

Questions 6 – 10

For each question, choose the correct answer.

The young people below all want to do art courses during their school summer holidays.

On the opposite page there are descriptions of eight art courses.

Decide which art course would be most suitable for the people below.

6  Asha wants to do an art course that also includes photography and has an exhibition of students' work. She'd like to stay at the place where the course is held.

7  Jack can only attend on weekdays and would like a course which focuses on painting people. He'd like to learn about the lives of famous artists.

8  Humera would like a course that is run by a professional artist where students learn how to paint animals. She can only go to classes in the morning.

9  Morio would like to learn how to make sculptures as well as paint, and needs advice on buying equipment. He wants a course which includes trips to various places so students can paint them.

10  Giulia wants a course that teaches her about painting landscapes. She'd like to learn about paintings from other countries and go on trips to galleries to look at professional artists' work.

TEST 3 READING

Summer art courses

A   Venture Art School

You'll learn about art from many countries on our summer course, with a focus on creating pictures of wildlife. The teacher is well-known painter Jeremy Silk, who will guide you through all you need to know about art. Runs weekdays only from 9.30 to midday for a whole month in the summer.

B   Artist's Dream

This year's summer course is run by professional painter Sally Green and well-known photographer Mike Riley. They're the perfect people to teach about their own special subject. The students' accommodation at the college is comfortable and cheap. Parents mustn't miss the end-of-course show of their children's amazing art.

C   Tempest Art Summer Course

Situated in a huge house in some of the country's finest landscapes, there's nowhere better to learn about painting the natural world than Tempest Art. Our students stay in the house, as well as learning there, and can choose to concentrate on creating pictures or sculptures of people, places or animals.

D   Brushwork

Our summer course is for anyone wanting to know about art from around the world. Artist and teacher Kate Figgis will teach you everything, from choosing the best brushes and paper, to creating perfect pictures of the local countryside. The price includes visits to see several exhibitions by well-known painters.

E   Palace Art School

Students just love having the opportunity to paint scenes in the city and countryside on our many half-day trips. Study the work and lives of artists such as Picasso and Pollock and be part of your own exhibition too, which friends and family are welcome to attend. Classes are 9 a.m. to noon daily.

F   Riley's Art Academy

If it's scenes from the local countryside you'd like to create, in paint or as sculpture, then Riley's is for you. We'll take you to some of the most beautiful places in the region to do it. All paints, brushes, etc. are provided, but we'll tell you which ones are best to get for you to use at home.

G   Xero's Art School

Whether it's photography, painting, drawing or sculpture you love, our summer school will provide you with what you want. Learn how to paint or photograph people – or perhaps animals are more your thing. Weekly trips to galleries are included. Classes run from late morning to 5 p.m., seven days a week.

H   Holly Granger's Art College

At Holly Granger's, we concentrate on painting the human face and body. Our summer school also covers other topics, from finding out about the greatest painters ever to studying international art. Classes are both mornings and afternoons, five days a week, with weekends free.

Part 3

Questions 11 – 15

For each question, choose the correct answer.

My unusual collection

Fourteen-year-old Johnny Paterson writes about collecting old mobile phones.

My hobby is collecting old mobile phones. Even people I don't know send me their old phones these days when they find out about my strange hobby. It all started when I was eight. I saw my parents using their mobiles all the time and I kept asking them if I could have one. My dad told the guy next door about this and one day he came round with a ten-year-old phone he no longer used. He thought letting me have it would stop me bothering my parents. Everyone at school thought it was great when I took it there the next day, even though it didn't actually work!

Everyone has a reason for collecting things. For some, it's because whatever they're collecting may be worth lots of money in the future. Others love having something that could be on display in a museum somewhere. That's certainly what attracts me to it. Compared to newer phones, mine are far less pleasant to look at. I often wonder what's inside them, as they're so much heavier than modern phones. I guess old batteries were much bigger.

Some people find my hobby a bit strange. I used to tell everyone about it, but some people just didn't know what to say, so they ended up feeling uncomfortable, which I'd rather avoid. I can completely understand – not everybody keeps over 150 old mobile phones in their bedroom! Most people find the fact it's unusual really interesting, and I'm proud to have such an unusual hobby.

My mum and dad put up some shelves to keep my collection on. Although there's probably space for a few more, and there are still some particular phones I'd like to find, I may give up collecting them before long. My dad recently gave me the coins he collected when he was my age and they look amazing. It's a far more expensive hobby but I really fancy having a go at it. I've spent more or less nothing on my phone collection so I've managed to save up quite a bit. We'll see!

11   Johnny was given the first phone in his collection by

   A   a neighbour.

   B   a relative.

   C   a classmate.

   D   a stranger.

12   Johnny says he collects old phones because

   A   he loves learning about how they work.

   B   they're more attractive than modern ones.

   C   it's like owning objects from a museum.

   D   they'll be valuable in a few years' time.

13   What does Johnny say about some people's attitudes towards his hobby?

   A   He's curious about why they find it so strange.

   B   He's keen to prevent anyone feeling embarrassed.

   C   He gets upset when they try to make him feel bad.

   D   He feels surprised that anyone finds it unusual.

14   Why does Johnny say he might stop collecting phones soon?

   A   He'll soon have all the models he wants.

   B   He has too little money to buy more.

   C   He'll have no more room for them.

   D   He wants to start collecting something else.

15   What would Johnny write in his diary?

A

> I never thought I'd end up with more than 150 phones when I got that first one when I was ten years old.

B

> When I took my first phone into my class, the teacher couldn't believe you could still make calls on something so old.

C

> I'm so grateful Mum and Dad support my hobby. I guess wanting to collect things is something I get from my dad.

D

> It's great that I've been able to make a bit of money by selling a few of the phones from my collection.

Part 4

Questions 16 – 20

Five sentences have been removed from the text below.

For each question, choose the correct answer.

There are three extra sentences which you do not need to use.

The world's first round-the-world flight powered by the Sun

In July 2016, Bertrand Piccard landed his plane, Solar Impulse 2, in the United Arab Emirates. He and his co-pilot André Borschberg had become the first people to fly around the world in a plane powered only by energy from the Sun. Solar Impulse 2 is a very unusual plane. Its wings are 72 m across. **16** [   ] Yet Solar Impulse 2 is over one-hundred times lighter.

The fastest flight around the world by plane was made in 1992. It took a little less than 32 hours to complete the 42 000 km journey. Solar Impulse 2, however, spent a total of 505 days finishing the trip, far longer than the five months originally planned for the project. The plane wasn't in the air for all of this time, of course. In fact, only 23 days were spent flying. **17** [   ] These delays were caused by technical problems, especially with the batteries.

Unlike typical planes, Solar Impulse 2 can stay in the air for a long time as it doesn't need to land for fuel. In one part of the journey over the Pacific Ocean, with Borschberg at the controls, the plane and its two pilots stayed in the air for almost five days without landing! **18** [   ] The previous best was only three days of continuous flight, made in a plane powered by traditional fuel.

Energy from the sun (solar power), is free and environmentally friendly. **19** [   ] So although it may have taken Solar Impulse 2 a long time, its flight had no negative effects on the environment. It's hoped that this achievement will encourage the use of more solar power worldwide.

Piccard and Borschberg are both from Switzerland. It's actually not the first time that Piccard has travelled around the world. **20** [   ] However, for this second trip he needed a pilot's licence, which took him over six years to get!

A   In doing this, it set a new world record.

B   The enormous size helps it to fly in this way but also causes problems.

C   This is about the same as the world's largest passenger plane.

D   As well as helping the environment, it was also reasonably fast.

E   In 1999, he made the same journey non-stop in a balloon.

F   At first, he was really pleased about it.

G   That's because pilots had to stop for long periods in various places.

H   It doesn't produce any of the damaging things that burning fuel creates.

Part 5

Questions 21 – 26

For each question, choose the correct answer.

___

The bicycle

The bicycle is one of the world's oldest forms of transport. In fact, the first successful bicycle was **(21)**.................... over two-hundred years ago, in 1817, by Baron Karl von Drais. He made it almost **(22)**.................... out of wood, even the wheels! This meant that it wasn't **(23)**.................... comfortable to ride, but on flat ground it could travel at twice the speed of someone walking.

Various different designs were used during the nineteenth century, **(24)**.................... machines with three and four wheels. Perhaps the most important **(25)**.................... of this time, however, was introduced by Scottish engineer, John Dunlop. He created the first tyres that were filled with air. With these, bicycles were far more comfortable to ride, so they quickly became more popular as a **(26)**.................... of transport. Since this time, the design of the bicycle has changed surprisingly little.

21	**A**	invented	**B**	started	**C**	discovered	**D**	intended
22	**A**	extremely	**B**	absolutely	**C**	fully	**D**	completely
23	**A**	mainly	**B**	particularly	**C**	mostly	**D**	largely
24	**A**	involving	**B**	containing	**C**	including	**D**	consisting
25	**A**	development	**B**	progress	**C**	increase	**D**	issue
26	**A**	style	**B**	way	**C**	method	**D**	technique

Part 6

Questions 27 – 32

For each question, write the correct answer.

Write **one** word for each gap.

Film review: *The Drive*

I saw a film called *The Drive* recently and I'd like to tell you about it. I think *The Drive* is **(27)**.................. of the best films I've ever seen. If you're into action, adventure and great characters, then I'm sure you **(28)**.................. love it too.

The story **(29)**.................. set about 100 years in the future. The heroes are two doctors, Jem and Mary, **(30)**.................. meet a young patient called Seb. Seb has a rare illness and must travel across the country to another hospital to get special help for it. Jem and Mary agree to drive Seb. (Seb can't travel on aeroplanes because **(31)**.................. his illness.) However, they must drive through many dangerous areas to get there.

I won't tell you what happens in **(32)**.................. end, but I'd like to suggest one thing. Go and see this film!

Part 1

You **must** answer this question.

Write your answer in about **100 words**.

Question 1

Read this email from your English-speaking friend Riley and the notes you have made.

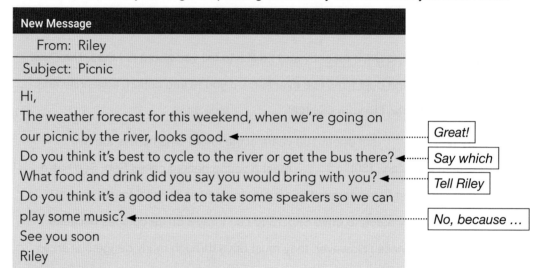

New Message
From: Riley
Subject: Picnic

Hi,
The weather forecast for this weekend, when we're going on our picnic by the river, looks good. ◄········· *Great!*
Do you think it's best to cycle to the river or get the bus there? ◄········· *Say which*
What food and drink did you say you would bring with you? ◄········· *Tell Riley*
Do you think it's a good idea to take some speakers so we can play some music? ◄········· *No, because …*
See you soon
Riley

Write your **email** to Riley using **all the notes**.

Part 2

Choose **one** of these questions.

Write your answer in about **100 words**.

Question 2

You see this announcement in your school English-language magazine.

> **Articles wanted!**
> **School clothes**
> What clothes do you usually wear for school?
> Do you think all students should wear school uniforms? What are the advantages and disadvantages of students wearing uniforms for school?
> The best articles answering these questions will be published next month.

Write your **article**.

Question 3

Your English teacher has asked you to write a story.

Your story must begin with this sentence.

When Billy saw the advertisement in the newspaper asking for young people to appear in a new film, he knew he had to apply.

Write your **story**.

Questions 1 – 7

For each question, choose the correct answer.

---

1   Where did the boy leave his phone?

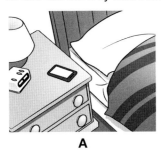  

           A   B   C

2   Which photo are they looking at?

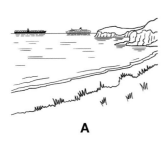 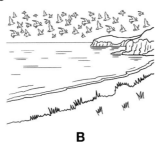 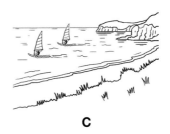

           A   B   C

3   How much did the boy pay for his football socks?

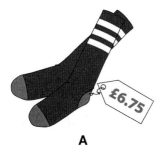 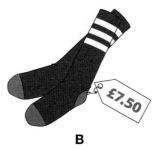 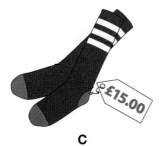

           A   B   C

4 What does the girl's pencil case look like?

A   B   C

5 What do they decide to watch on TV?

A   B   C

6 What event did the girl see at the weekend?

A   B   C

7 What should the students write about for homework?

A   B   C

Questions 8 – 13

For each question, choose the correct answer.

---

8   You will hear a boy telling a friend about his holiday.
     What did he enjoy most about it?

   A   the sort of people he met

   B   the up-to-date accommodation

   C   the range of organised activities

9   You will hear a girl telling a friend about a volleyball match she played in.
     How does she feel about it?

   A   satisfied with her own performance

   B   grateful for the support of her team mates

   C   impressed by the skills of players on both sides

10   You will hear two friends talking about a website they use for homework.
     What do they agree about it?

   A   how simple it is to use

   B   how much you can learn from it

   C   how clearly things are explained on it

11   You will hear a girl telling a friend about a musical show she went to.
     What did she think of it?

   A   The story wasn't realistic enough.

   B   The music wasn't very well played.

   C   The jokes weren't particularly funny.

12   You will hear two friends talking about some homework.
     What is the girl doing?

   A   explaining how she approached it

   B   suggesting that they do it together

   C   admitting that she didn't understand it

13   You will hear a boy telling a friend about a book he read.
     What did he like best about it?

   A   the age of the characters

   B   how exciting the story was

   C   what it made him think about

Part 3

For each question, write the correct answer in the gap. Write **one** or **two words** or a **number** or a **date** or a **time**.

You will hear a boy called Josh giving a presentation about quad biking.

Quad biking

Josh says that the size of the quad bike's **(14)**_____ is the best thing about it.

Josh spent **(15)**_____ learning how to drive the quad bike safely.

For Josh, driving through a **(16)**_____ was the most challenging part of the session.

Josh was pleased that the weather was **(17)**_____ on the day he went.

The quad biking centre is on the road that goes to the **(18)**_____ .

To book a session, go online at www. **(19)**_____.com

For each question, choose the correct answer.

You will hear an interview with a girl called Mandy Thornhill, who is talking about her school's radio station.

20   Mandy explains that her school's radio station

   A   can only be heard in the school building.

   B   is sometimes played during classes.

   C   was the first one in her home area.

21   How did Mandy get involved with the radio station?

   A   She suggested the idea originally.

   B   She responded to a request for help.

   C   She was chosen by a member of staff.

22   How did the students learn to operate the equipment?

   A   The company that made it gave them training.

   B   They studied the instructions very carefully.

   C   They found somebody able to show them.

23   What does Mandy say about preparing for her programme?

   A   Most weeks it doesn't take long.

   B   She never feels she spends enough time on it.

   C   She doesn't like it when she has to interview someone.

24   How did Mandy feel about her first live broadcast?

   A   It was embarrassing to make mistakes.

   B   It was much easier than she expected.

   C   It was hard to think of things to say.

25   What does Mandy say about the radio station and studying?

   A   It makes it hard to finish all her homework on time.

   B   She's able to keep the two things separate.

   C   It's taught her some relevant life skills.

Part 1 (2–3 minutes)

Phase 1

- What's your name?
- How old are you?
- Where do you live?
- Who do you live with?

Phase 2

- What do you enjoy doing in the evening? (Why?)
- Do you often go to the cinema? (Why?/Why not?)
- Where do you usually do your homework? (Why?)
- What do you like doing when you go on holiday? (Why?)
- What type of food do you like? (Why?)
- Who's your favourite teacher at school? (Why?)
- Tell us about your best friend.
- Do you listen to music in the evenings? (Why?/Why not?)

Part 2 (2–3 minutes)

3A Shopping

Now I'd like each of you to talk on your own about something.
I'm going to give each of you a photograph and I'd like you to talk about it.
A, here is your photograph. It shows **people shopping**.
[*Turn to photograph 3A on page 193.*]
B, you just listen.
A, please tell us what you can see in the photograph.

🕐 about 1 minute

Thank you.

3B Cycling

B, here is your photograph.
It shows **people cycling**.
[*Turn to photograph 3B on page 197.*]
A, you just listen.
B, please tell us what you can see in the photograph.

🕐 about 1 minute

Thank you.

Part 3 (2–3 minutes)

Now, in this part of the test you're going to talk about something together for about two minutes. I'm going to describe a situation to you.

[*Turn to the task on page 202.*]

A girl's parents and grandparents want to do something special with her on her fourteenth birthday. They want to do something they can all enjoy.

Here are some things they could do together.

Talk together about the different things they could do, and say which would be best for everyone.

All right? Now talk together.

 2–3 minutes

Thank you.

Part 4 (2–3 minutes)

- What do you enjoy doing on your birthday? (Why?)
- Do you prefer spending your birthday with your family or your friends? (Why?)
- If your birthday is on a school day, do you celebrate then or at the weekend? (Why?)
- Is it important to always celebrate birthdays? (Why?/Why not?)
- Do you think it's necessary to spend a lot of money celebrating a birthday? (Why?/Why not?)

 2–3 minutes

Thank you.

Part 1

Questions 1 – 5

For each question, choose the correct answer.

1

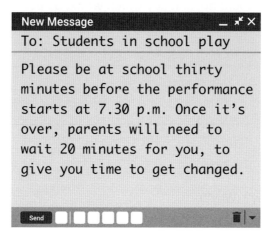

Students in the play should

A arrive twenty minutes early so they can get changed.

B tell their parents that the performance lasts thirty minutes.

C ask parents to collect them twenty minutes after it ends.

2

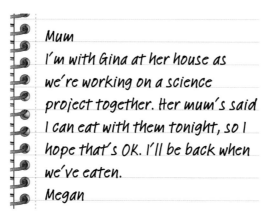

A Megan will go home for dinner after doing a science project at Gina's house.

B Megan is doing homework with Gina and will return home after her evening meal.

C Megan has just eaten and is going to do her science homework with Gina.

3

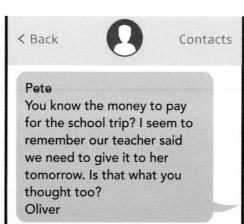

Oliver is

A checking the information he has about the school trip is correct.

B reminding Pete to bring the money for the school trip tomorrow.

C asking how much money he needs to bring for the school trip.

4

School sports day

Due to bad weather, this will now take place on Tuesday of next week instead of this Friday. Anyone willing to help set up events should tell one of the sports teachers.

A   Tuesday's weather forecast is bad so sports day has changed to a different day.

B   On Friday, students and sports teachers will arrange things for next Tuesday's sports day.

C   Sports teachers need volunteers to give them a hand organising next Tuesday's competitions.

5

Our newspapers are for all customers.

Please do not remove them from the café.

A   The café provides newspapers that any customer is allowed to read.

B   Newspapers are for sale to any café customer who wants one.

C   Customers are reminded to take their newspapers when leaving the café.

Part 2

Questions 6 – 10

For each question, choose the correct answer.

The young people below are all looking for film websites.

On the opposite page there are eight descriptions of film websites.

Decide which website would be most suitable for the people below.

6  Brad wants to read reviews of the latest films. He'd also like to be able to see free films on the website and find out about drama courses he can apply for.

7  Sonny would like to watch interviews with famous actors and get advice about creating her own film. She wants a website which has competitions she can enter.

8  Serge would like to find a website he can upload his own films onto. He'd like to be able to read biographies of well-known actors and find adverts for acting work.

9  Alicia would like to read articles about how famous films were made and vote for her favourite actors and films. She wants a site that has film equipment for sale.

10  Stelios wants a website which explains the duties of everyone that's involved in making a film. He'd like to read advice given by famous actors, and reviews of TV programmes as well as films.

Film websites

A **www.rileyfilm.net**

This website is for serious film lovers. Although there are the usual film reviews and actor interviews, its most original feature is the message board for anyone looking for acting jobs. The site has life stories of the most famous actors and you can even post your own short movies for others to comment on.

B **www.priusfilm.net**

Offering reviews of the latest movies, games and TV programmes, this is a very popular site. There's a section on making your own films, as well as biographies of many actors and directors. The site allows users to post adverts for selling any unwanted equipment.

C **www.gammafilmworld.com**

Whether its tips on acting by the world's best-known stars or suggestions for how to make a movie at home you want, this site has it all. There are videos of the site's experts talking to well-known film stars and you can also win trips to Hollywood, cameras and other great prizes here.

D **www.actingnormal.com**

If you've made your own short films, why not upload them onto this great site? There's also plenty of advice for improving your film-making skills. Drama courses all around the country are also listed here, and there are competitions to win cinema tickets and loads more.

E **www.sunnyfilms.net**

This site has regularly updated opinion on not just recently released movies, but also the latest television series. You can also find out what all the people in the list of credits at the end of a film actually do. There are suggestions by the biggest stars about how to get into acting too.

F **www.blastoffmovies.com**

This great site has many job adverts for acting work for all ages, in addition to expert opinion on all recent movies and TV drama. There are detailed descriptions of every acting school and class in the country. There's no charge for watching the many old movies available here.

G **www.jedthefilmfan.com**

You can vote for your movie and actor of the year on this popular site, as well as being able to watch classic old films for free here. You can see film clips of famous actors being interviewed and read about them in their biographies on the site.

H **www.myfilmcentral.net**

If you've ever wondered what everyone involved in making films does, then this is the site for you! Learn about the techniques directors of great films used to make their work and choose who you think should win the site's famous actor and film of the year competitions. You can also buy video cameras and other stuff here.

Part 3

Questions 11 – 15

For each question, choose the correct answer.

Student expedition to Antarctica

Fifteen-year-old Melanie Brenner writes about her trip to the coldest place on Earth.

Four weeks ago, I was on Antarctica! I went there with twenty other students on a three-week educational programme, and we saw some of the most amazing wildlife on Earth. I decided to try and get a place after seeing a programme about how Antarctica was affected by climate change. I thought it'd be a great way to see directly the effect it's having. It was more amazing than I'd imagined and I'd love to go back, perhaps as a scientist in one of the teams that work there.

I was surprised by how little life there was there. Documentaries show landscapes covered in penguins and seas full of whales, but of course the film-makers stay there for months to film so many. I saw some, but not in the numbers I'd expected. As it's the coldest place on Earth, I also thought it'd be well below freezing even in summer, but that wasn't always the case. There's plenty of sun because it's light all the time, which I hadn't got used to even by the time we left. I'd read how many visitors Antarctica gets these days, so seeing several boatloads of visitors didn't seem that strange.

In our first group session, we all had to say why we'd come on the expedition. There were twenty students and twenty different explanations! Even though we were all a bit shy, we made friends with each other from day one. You often get a few people in a group who start telling the others what to do. Fortunately, this wasn't the case with us. We've set up a social media group which we're all posting messages onto. It's nice, as we've become pretty close.

In some ways it's been a relief to be home and a school student again, as the routine is so familiar and I was away for such a long time. It's been nice to see my mates again too, although for some reason they change the subject whenever I start talking about my trip. Maybe they're jealous, which is a bit sad. Anyway, I've become much more serious about helping the environment. I can understand why we do things that harm it, as I've done them all myself. It's not about blaming anyone but about changing people's habits.

11 Melanie applied for the expedition to Antarctica because she wanted to

    A   see lots of the animals there.

    B   help with scientific research.

    C   experience something unusual.

    D   learn about global warming.

12 What did Melanie find most unusual about Antarctica?

    A   the 24-hour daylight

    B   how cold summer there was

    C   how much wildlife there was

    D   the number of tourists

13 What does Melanie say about the other students on the expedition?

    A   Some of them were rather bossy.

    B   They were all there for similar reasons.

    C   Everyone has kept in touch with each other.

    D   It took time to get to know them.

14 Since getting home from the expedition, Melanie has felt

    A   ashamed of what people are doing to our planet.

    B   disappointed with the reactions of her friends.

    C   annoyed that she didn't go on a longer trip.

    D   miserable about being back at school.

15 What would another expedition member say about Melanie?

    A

> Melanie was very angry with people for causing the environmental problems we learnt about in Antarctica, which was strange for someone so shy.

    B

> It was such a pleasure spending those months in Antarctica with Melanie, especially watching all those penguins and whales with her.

    C

> Melanie didn't take what we were doing in Antarctica particularly seriously and seemed to miss being back at home quite a lot.

    D

> I hope Melanie's dream comes true and she can qualify as an environmental scientist and go back to do research in Antarctica.

Part 4

Questions 16 – 20

Five sentences have been removed from the text below.

For each question, choose the correct answer.

There are three extra sentences which you do not need to use.

The best ways to learn another language

There are thousands of different websites offering advice about the best ways to learn languages. Some of these claim that you can learn the language of your choice in only a few weeks. **16** [ ] Therefore, expecting to be fluent in only a few weeks is clearly not realistic.

The thought of learning a language can be quite frightening, especially as it seems such a huge task. Most people who think of doing so simply never try, as they listen to that voice in their heads that keeps telling them they can't do it because it's too much work. This same problem makes giving up once you've started very likely too. **17** [ ] When you achieve each one, you feel good and this helps to remove any feelings of fear you may have.

Most language experts agree it's better to learn new words and grammar using topics that interest you. Reading long lists of words is definitely not an efficient way of learning new vocabulary. **18** [ ] Reading those same words in an article about a subject that you find interesting, however, won't send you to sleep and is a much better way to remember them.

Many people will happily tell you that you can only learn a language really well when you're young, preferably a child. **19** [ ] Instead, just carry on learning because there's plenty of evidence to show that, although adults learn in different ways from children, they can become just as good.

Learning more about your own language can actually help you when it comes to trying a new language. Learning to use anything well involves gaining understanding of how it works, and languages are no different. **20** [ ] You can then use what you've learnt when trying to develop your skills in the new language.

A   It's of course easier to do this using a language you already know well.

B   That's why it's important to break your learning up into small, clear goals.

C   Therefore you'll be able to remember these new words forever.

D   Most people also find it extremely boring.

E   The longer you spend following these steps, the better your understanding will be.

F   However, language learning is something that continues for the whole of your life.

G   So your first language can actually make this more difficult.

H   Don't listen to them because it's simply not true.

Part 5

Questions 21 – 26

For each question, choose the correct answer.

The Catatumbo lightning

The Catatumbo lightning is a natural event that takes place in Venezuela, South America. The lightning comes from storm clouds over the place where the Catatumbo River **(21)**................... into Lake Maracaibo. There's nothing **(22)**................... unusual about lightning, of course. It is a common **(23)**................... in many places around the world. What makes the Catatumbo lightning so special is how **(24)**................... it is seen. While storms and lightning may happen a few times a year in many places, at Catatumbo they take **(25)**................... an incredible 140 to 160 times every year. In addition, once the lightning storms start, they can **(26)**................... for up to 10 hours, with lightning appearing as many as 280 times per hour! No one really knows why there's so much lightning in one single place.

21	**A**	travels	**B**	moves	**C**	pours	**D**	flows
22	**A**	mainly	**B**	especially	**C**	totally	**D**	completely
23	**A**	scene	**B**	display	**C**	sight	**D**	view
24	**A**	frequently	**B**	usually	**C**	normally	**D**	generally
25	**A**	off	**B**	part	**C**	up	**D**	place
26	**A**	hold	**B**	last	**C**	live	**D**	keep

Questions 27 – 32

For each question, write the correct answer.

Write **one** word for each gap.

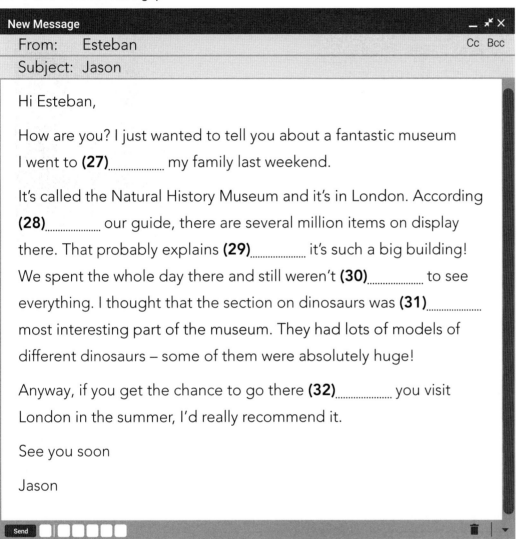

New Message   — ⤢ ✕

From: Esteban   Cc Bcc
Subject: Jason

Hi Esteban,

How are you? I just wanted to tell you about a fantastic museum I went to **(27)**................. my family last weekend.

It's called the Natural History Museum and it's in London. According **(28)**................. our guide, there are several million items on display there. That probably explains **(29)**............... it's such a big building! We spent the whole day there and still weren't **(30)**............... to see everything. I thought that the section on dinosaurs was **(31)**............... most interesting part of the museum. They had lots of models of different dinosaurs – some of them were absolutely huge!

Anyway, if you get the chance to go there **(32)**............... you visit London in the summer, I'd really recommend it.

See you soon

Jason

Send ☐ ☐ ☐ ☐ ☐ ☐   🗑 | ▾

Part 1

You **must** answer this question.
Write your answer in about **100 words**.

Question 1

Read this email from your English-speaking friend Ellis and the notes you have made.

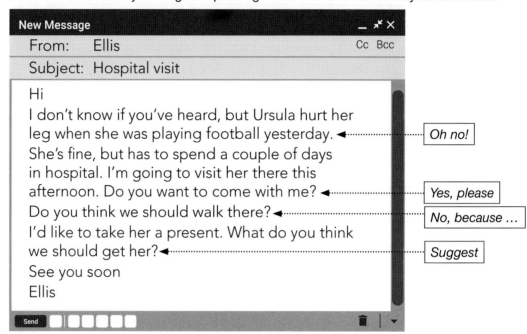

New Message — ⤴ ✕

From: Ellis   Cc Bcc

Subject: Hospital visit

Hi
I don't know if you've heard, but Ursula hurt her
leg when she was playing football yesterday. ◀········· *Oh no!*
She's fine, but has to spend a couple of days
in hospital. I'm going to visit her there this
afternoon. Do you want to come with me? ◀········· *Yes, please*
Do you think we should walk there? ◀········· *No, because …*
I'd like to take her a present. What do you think
we should get her? ◀········· *Suggest*
See you soon
Ellis

Send

Write your **email** to Ellis using **all the notes**.

Part 2

Choose **one** of these questions.
Write your answer in about **100 words**.

Question 2

You see this announcement on an English-language website.

> **Holidays**
> Everyone loves going on holiday, but where's the best place for the whole family to
> have fun together – the seaside, a city or somewhere else?
> Should you try to do lots of things while you're on holiday, or do very little?
> Write an article answering these questions and we'll put it on our website!

Write your **article**.

Question 3

Your English teacher has asked you to write a story.

Your story must begin with this sentence.

Casey couldn't wait for the train she was on to arrive at its destination.

Write your **story**.

Part I

Questions 1 – 7

For each question, choose the correct answer.

---

1   What will the weather be like for the football match?

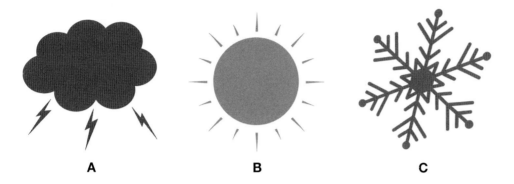

A   B   C

2   What has the girl forgotten to bring to school?

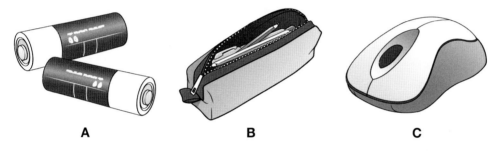

A   B   C

3   What time does the bus leave?

A   B   C

4 Which cake does the girl decide to have?

A   B   C

5 Where should the students go at break time?

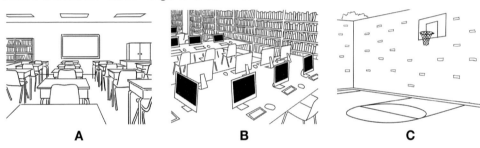

A   B   C

6 Which musical instrument is the boy learning?

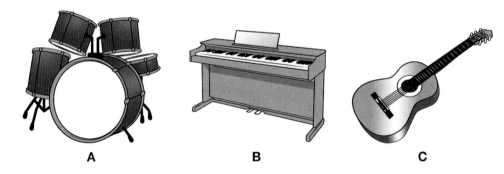

A   B   C

7 Which activity did the girl do at the weekend?

A   B   C

Questions 8 – 13

For each question, choose the correct answer.

8   You will hear two friends talking about a TV quiz show.
    What did the boy feel about it?

    A   surprised by how hard the questions were

    B   disappointed that it wasn't more serious

    C   amused by the people taking part in it

9   You will hear two friends talking about their classrooms at school.
    What do they agree about?

    A   none of them needs painting

    B   only some of them should be painted

    C   they should all be painted to look the same

10 You will hear a boy telling a friend about a new shopping mall.
    What impressed him about it?

    A   the range of things to buy

    B   the attitude of the staff

    C   the value for money

11 You will hear two friends talking about a drama club they go to.
    What do they like best about it?

    A   the skills they learn there

    B   the people they meet there

    C   the things they discuss there

12 You will hear a girl telling a friend about a class presentation she has to give.
    How is she feeling about it?

    A   worried about how much to practise

    B   nervous about using the equipment

    C   unhappy about her choice of topic

13 You will hear two friends talking about a book they've read.
    What do they both think?

    A   it has very realistic characters

    B   it must be based on a true story

    C   it's impossible to predict the ending

Questions 14 – 19

For each question, write the correct answer in the gap. Write **one** or **two words** or a **number** or a **date** or a **time**.

You will hear a girl called Emily giving a presentation about a class trip to a zoo.

Class trip to a zoo

In the zoo, there are **(14)**................. different species of very rare animals.

Emily really liked the work of the **(15)**................. she met there.

Emily enjoyed the **(16)**................. lesson they had about kangaroos.

After lunch, Emily chose a session about **(17)**................. .

Emily's group studied the behaviour of some **(18)**................. .

The school website has some data and a **(19)**................. of the trip.

Part 4

Questions 20 – 25

For each question, choose the correct answer.

You will hear an interview with a girl called Mara who started a book club at her school.

20   Mara first thought of starting a school book club after

    A   she read about one online.

    B   one of her parents suggested it.

    C   somebody at school told her about one.

21   What does Mara say about the club meetings?

    A   They're always led by one of her teachers.

    B   A different person picks the book for each one.

    C   Students have to prepare answers to questions.

22   Mara thinks it's better if the club reads books which

    A   nobody in the group has read.

    B   everybody in the group has heard of.

    C   somebody in the group knows and loves.

23   Mara says that if some members don't like a book,

    A   she tries to change their mind.

    B   then they don't have to finish reading it.

    C   it can make the meetings more interesting.

24   Mara enjoys it most when members of the book club

    A   share ideas for stories of their own.

    B   get in touch with the author of the book.

    C   watch a film based on the book they're reading.

25   Mara advises anyone interested in starting a school book club to

    A   give members different responsibilities.

    B   decide the type of novels they're going to read.

    C   encourage new members to join from time to time.

Part 1 (2–3 minutes)

Phase 1

- What's your name?
- How old are you?
- Where do you live?
- Who do you live with?

Phase 2

- Do you often watch films at home? (Why?/Why not?)
- Is there a subject you don't like at school? (Why?/Why not?)
- What's your favourite day of the week? (Why?)
- Is there a country you'd really like to visit on holiday? (Why?)
- Do you prefer hot or cold weather? (Why?)
- Would you like to have music lessons? (Why?/Why not?)
- Do you use your mobile phone at school? (Why?/Why not?)
- Do you enjoy reading? (Why?/Why not?)

Part 2 (2–3 minutes)

4A Spending time together after school
Now I'd like each of you to talk on your own about something.
I'm going to give each of you a photograph and I'd like you to talk about it.
A, here is your photograph. It shows **people spending time together after school**.
[Turn to photograph 4A on page 193.]
B, you just listen.
A, please tell us what you can see in the photograph.

🕐 about 1 minute

Thank you.

4B Having a snack
B, here is your photograph. It shows **people having a snack**.
[Turn to photograph 4B on page 197.]
A, you just listen.
B, please tell us what you can see in the photograph.

🕐 about 1 minute

Thank you.

Part 3 (2–3 minutes)

Now, in this part of the test you're going to talk about something together for about two minutes. I'm going to describe a situation to you.

[*Turn to the task on page 203.*]

Some students want to buy a gift for their maths teacher who is retiring. They want to buy something but they don't want to spend a lot of money.

Here are some gifts they could buy.

Talk together about the different gifts they could buy for their teacher, and say which would be best.

All right? Now talk together.

🕐 2–3 minutes

Thank you.

Part 4 (2–3 minutes)

- Have you ever given a teacher a gift? (Why?/Why not?)
- Is it a good idea to give a teacher a gift when he or she retires? (Why?/Why not?)
- Do you prefer to give gifts, or to receive them? (Why?)
- Do you think it's easy to choose gifts for other people? (Why?/Why not?)
- Are expensive gifts always the best gifts? (Why?/Why not?)

🕐 2–3 minutes

Thank you.

Part 1

Questions 1 – 5

For each question, choose the correct answer.

1

24-hour access needed to building. Bikes attached here will be removed.

£25 fine.

A   It's OK to leave bikes here if you pay £25.

B   No one is allowed to leave their bike here.

C   Bikes can be left here for a maximum of 24 hours.

2

Mum

I'm afraid the fridge broke just before I left for school this morning. The food's fine – I asked the neighbours for help and they'll look after it until our fridge is fixed.

Libby

A   Libby is telling her mum how she solved a problem at home.

B   Libby is apologising for breaking the fridge this morning.

C   Libby is explaining why their neighbours needed help earlier today.

3

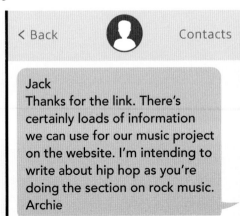

< Back   Contacts

Jack
Thanks for the link. There's certainly loads of information we can use for our music project on the website. I'm intending to write about hip hop as you're doing the section on rock music.
Archie

A   Archie is sending Jack website details and a suggestion of what to write about.

B   Archie wants Jack to send him some information about hip hop for their music project.

C   Archie is informing Jack what he'll do for their music project, using the website.

4

New Message   _ ⤢ ✕

To: Sarah   Cc Bcc

From: Justine

Did I hear you saying to Lisa that you've got a new bike? How do you fancy going out for a ride this weekend? We could invite Lisa along as well.

Send 🗑 ▼

Justine wants to

A   organise a ride with Sarah and ask Lisa to come too.

B   know if Sarah and Lisa can help her choose a bike.

C   invite Sarah and Lisa round to look at her new bike.

5

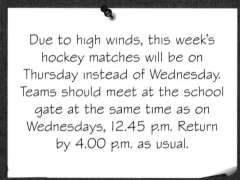

Due to high winds, this week's hockey matches will be on Thursday instead of Wednesday. Teams should meet at the school gate at the same time as on Wednesdays, 12.45 p.m. Return by 4.00 p.m. as usual.

A   Members of the school hockey teams will set off for matches later than usual.

B   The school has moved hockey matches to a different day because of bad weather.

C   Hockey matches that were planned to take place on Thursday this week are cancelled.

Part 2

Questions 6 – 10

For each question, choose the correct answer.

The young people below all want to do a cookery course in the long school holiday.

On the opposite page there are descriptions of eight cookery courses.

Decide which course would be most suitable for the people below.

6  Parvin would like to do a general cookery course with her parents but they can only attend a course in the mornings. She wants a course that takes place near public transport links.

7  Kasper wants a course that's aimed at vegetarians and that can organise accommodation for him nearby. He already has some experience of cooking.

8  Gina wants a course that focuses on preparing desserts. She'd like a course that includes competitions, and which only has a small number of other students on it.

9  Ding would like a course that's suitable for beginners and that includes work experience in a working kitchen. He'd like to learn how to cook food from many different countries.

10  Melanie would like to do a course that includes going on trips and that is run by well-known chefs. She'd especially like to learn how to make bread and cakes.

Cookery courses

A Central Cookery School

This course for teenagers is for experts and beginners alike, especially if preparing sweet dishes like cakes, pies and fruit salads is your thing. Places are limited to just six students, so book early! As well as tasting trips to local restaurants, there are prizes for whoever creates the best dish each day.

B The Cookery College

Run by professional cooks, Jenny and Mike Halliday, the full-day courses here are aimed at teenagers without much experience in the kitchen who want to attend with parents. They are suitable for both meat eaters and vegetarians, and there's a daily competition for the person who produces the tastiest cooking. Accommodation arranged on request.

C Food for Life

Learn to make a wide range of dishes from many different countries with ex-TV chef Judith Makepeace. Baking bread, pies and cakes is also covered in the course, as well as creating other types of dessert. Close to both the train and bus stations. All day on weekdays.

D Cook and a Half

You're sure to recognise the cooks who teach our course for teenagers from their hit online video channel, Bake Online. The cake and bread-making in their videos is also the focus of the course. They organise visits to local restaurants so you can watch chefs at work in a busy kitchen.

E Can Cook, Will Cook

Open to students of all ages and abilities, summer courses here run from 9 a.m. to midday daily. You'll learn how to make the best meals ever with celebrity chefs Harry Hunter and Elaine Mitchell. Bus stops and rail station are just a five-minute walk away.

F The Cook's Challenge

You'll be able to make international vegetarian food as well as being a professional chef once you've finished this course. Aimed at the less experienced cook, there are only five students per course, to make sure you get lots of attention from the well-known chefs who run the courses.

G Future Chefs

Every chef should know how to make food from all over the world, and that's exactly what you'll learn here. Aimed at those with few cooking skills, the classes will build your confidence until you're ready to find out what life as a chef is really like by helping out in a real restaurant kitchen.

H The Recipe Centre

Perfect for teenagers who have already spent time developing their cooking abilities, this course will take you to the next level. None of the dishes you'll create contain meat. The Recipe Centre can even arrange somewhere to stay while you're on the course. Next to the train station.

Part 3

Questions 11 – 15

For each question, choose the correct answer.

Learning how to dive
Fourteen-year-old Henry Unsworth writes about his experiences.

Some of my friends have wanted to try diving for a long time. Although I'm a strong swimmer, I'd always been frightened of deep water. So I'd never considered going diving, even though I knew seeing all the fish would be amazing. I finally got so annoyed at being too terrified to swim in the sea on holiday that I asked if I could do a diving course. My mum and dad thought it would help me too, so I booked a three-day course.

There were six students on the course and we practised in a local pool. We had some classroom sessions on safety and managing stress first, then tried on the equipment. It looked quite confusing but I got used to it surprisingly quickly in the water. I was amazed how hard it was to judge how much air to put into or let out of my diving jacket, though. This is how you move up and down in the water. It's almost silent underwater when you're swimming, but diving is just the opposite because of the noise of your breathing.

Our teacher, Amy, was very experienced. We spent time in the classroom with her, learning about each new skill before we practised it in the pool. She made everything sound so easy, but it took a lot of practice to get it right, so I'm grateful we had to keep doing tasks until we could do them almost without thinking. This took some people longer than others, but she'd stay with them until they could do whatever it was we were learning, which was really important.

When we did our first sea dive, we were lucky that the water was really clear, as it's often hard to see more than a few metres. I soon wished I'd bought a thicker wetsuit though, as it was much colder than I'd expected. You could feel the waves underwater, which we'd never experienced in the pool, but I found it quite relaxing. We had to dive with a 'buddy' – like an underwater partner – and couldn't go more than a metre or two away from them. To my surprise, I had a really great dive!

11   Why did Henry decide to learn how to dive?

    A   to add excitement to his life

    B   to please his parents

    C   to deal with a fear

    D   to achieve an ambition

12   What surprised Henry when he first went diving in the pool?

    A   how calm he felt

    B   how quiet it was underwater

    C   how complicated the equipment was

    D   how difficult it was to control your depth

13   What does Henry say about his teacher?

    A   It was annoying that she focused so much on some students.

    B   He's glad she made everyone repeat certain exercises.

    C   Her explanations weren't always very clear.

    D   She spent the right amount of time in the classroom.

14   What did Henry find most difficult about diving in the sea?

    A   the temperature of the water

    B   being able to see very little

    C   the way the water moved

    D   being far from other divers

15   What would one of Henry's friends say about him?

    A

> Henry wanted to go on a diving course for a long time before he finally got enough courage to do one.

    B

> Henry had to fight against his parents' wishes for a long time before they let him do a diving course.

    C

> Henry was really pleased with his diving instructor and he didn't have a negative thing to say about her.

    D

> It took so long for Henry to learn how to swim that I'd already done the diving course by the time he could do it.

Questions 16 – 20

Five sentences have been removed from the text below.

For each question, choose the correct answer.

There are three extra sentences which you do not need to use.

The teenage businesswoman

Tiffany Patterson has run her own beauty business since she was only fifteen years old. She has recently employed two members of staff to help her out, so her business is growing fast. 'It was quite strange interviewing people for the jobs,' explains Tiffany. **16** [   ] Despite this, Tiffany says her new employees treat her with a lot of respect.

Tiffany learnt to put make-up on others in her early teenage years, by helping out at her aunt's beauty business. She'd already set up her own business by the time she began a part-time beauty course at college, aged sixteen. 'I'd have beauty classes in the morning then would do make-up for family and friends in the afternoon,' says Tiffany. **17** [   ] Everyone liked what Tiffany did and she was soon earning a reasonable amount of money for a sixteen-year-old.

What's even more amazing is that Tiffany finds reading and writing very hard. 'I have something called dyslexia. Lots of people have this, but it makes reading and writing a real challenge,' explains Tiffany. **18** [   ] The help she received enabled her to pass the course easily and now she works at her business full time.

'I got a place on the high street of my town about six months ago,' says Tiffany. **19** [   ] So that's when she decided to employ two other staff. This has allowed her to offer many more services to her customers: 'They can both do things that I never learnt at college,' explains Tiffany, 'so we make a great team!'

As for the future, Tiffany has big plans. 'I'd like to sell a wider range of beauty products and open places in other towns and cities too,' says Tiffany. **20** [   ] Looking at how well Tiffany has done so far, it's sure to be a great success.

A 'I was soon so busy that I couldn't do everything myself.'

B 'They've already been extremely helpful.'

C 'So I was trying things I'd learnt at college later the same day.'

D 'I'm really looking forward to it starting soon.'

E 'Having a chain like this would greatly increase what I could earn.'

F 'They were all so much older than me and had much more experience.'

G 'It was because of these difficulties that I had to give up.'

H 'But the college provided lots of extra support with this difficulty.'

Part 5

Questions 21 – 26

For each question, choose the correct answer.

The first plants on the Moon

The Moon is not a very good place to have a garden! Daytime temperatures there are around 130°C, while at night, they **(21)** .... as low as –170°C. But in January 2019, Chinese scientists **(22)** .... that they had successfully grown plants on the Moon for the first time ever.

The small Chinese spaceship that was carrying the plants **(23)** .... on the side of the Moon that we can't ever see from Earth. It was carrying cotton seeds – the tiny objects that cotton plants grow from – in a special glass box. Scientists could **(24)** .... the temperature inside the box. With plenty of light **(25)** .... onto the plants, after a few days, the cotton seeds started to grow.

(26) .... , just a few days later, the plants died when it became night-time on that part of the Moon. One freezing-cold night on the Moon lasts an incredible fourteen Earth days!

21	A	cut	B	decrease	C	fall	D	reduce
22	A	announced	B	described	C	told	D	informed
23	A	stepped	B	reached	C	entered	D	landed
24	A	run	B	control	C	use	D	organise
25	A	racing	B	flying	C	burning	D	shining
26	A	Urgently	B	Extremely	C	Unfortunately	D	Absolutely

Part 6

Questions 27 – 32

For each question, write the correct answer.

Write **one** word for each gap.

Blog post on a book about basketball

In this week's blog post, I'd like to tell you about a book I read recently. The book's called *My Life in Basketball*, and it **(27)** .... written last year by the American professional basketball player, Tina Martinez.

If you've read my blog before, you'll know just how **(28)** .... I love basketball – it's my favourite sport – so I really enjoy reading books about it. I actually read the whole book in **(29)** .... than a week – about four days, I think.

I'm sure Tina Martinez could be a great journalist when she finally gives **(30)** .... playing basketball because she's a really good writer. As **(31)** .... as lots of information about Tina's life, there are some great pictures in the book.

I'd really recommend this book. In fact, I gave it to a friend of **(32)** .... last week and she says she is enjoying it too.

Part 1

You **must** answer this question.

Write your answer in about **100 words**.

Question 1

Read the email from your English-speaking friend Francis and the notes you have made.

New Message
From: Francis
Subject: School play
Hi
It's not long now until the performance of our school play and I'm feeling really worried about it. ◄ ······································· *Oh dear!*
What can I do to help me feel less nervous? ◄ ······························· *Suggest …*
I'm finding it hard to remember what I have to say. How did you learn all the words your character has to say? ◄ ······· *Explain to Francis*
Can I come to your house after school tomorrow so we can practise together? ◄ ······································· *No, but …*
Write back soon.
Francis

Write your **email** to Francis using **all the notes**.

Part 2

Choose **one** of these questions.

Write your answer in about **100 words**.

Question 2

You see this announcement on an English-language website.

> **The perfect weekend**
> We want your ideas about your perfect weekend.
> Would you spend it with friends, with family, with both or on your own?
> What would you do? Why?
> Write an article answering these questions and we'll put it on our website!

Write your **article**.

Question 3

Your English teacher has asked you to write a story.

Your story must begin with this sentence.

Sophie had never noticed the unusual little shop before, so she decided to go in.

Write your **story**.

Part 1

Questions 1 – 7

For each question, choose the correct answer.

1   What will the girl make for the party?

A   B   C

2   What will the boy write about for homework?

A   B   C

3   What time is the boy's appointment?

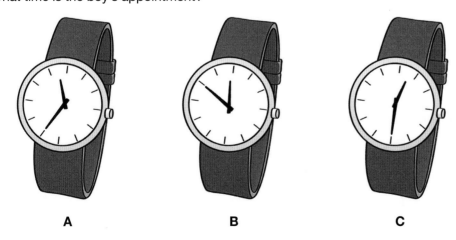

A   B   C

4 Which photo will the girl enter for the competition?

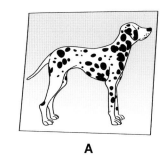

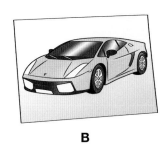

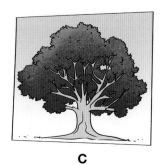

A

B

C

5 What did the boy buy in the museum shop?

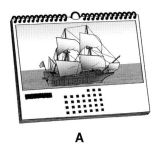

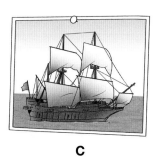

A

B

C

6 What can the girl see from her window?

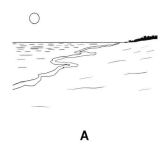

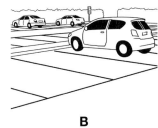

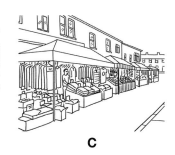

A

B

C

7 Where is the girl going first this afternoon?

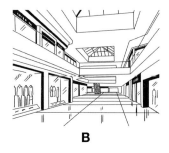

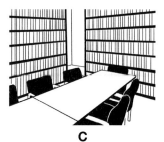

A

B

C

Questions 8 – 13

For each question, choose the correct answer.

8   You will hear two friends talking about cycling in their town.
     What does the girl like about it?

    A   It helps the environment.

    B   It's a useful form of exercise.

    C   It's an efficient way of travelling.

9   You will hear a boy telling a friend about some homework.
     How does he feel about it?

    A   sure that he won't finish on time

    B   sorry that he can't do other things

    C   annoyed because he can't get any help

10   You will hear two friends talking about the weekend.
     Why doesn't the girl want to go shopping?

    A   She doesn't have enough money.

    B   The centre will be too crowded.

    C   It will waste too much time.

11   You will hear two friends talking about a computer game.
     What do they both think about it?

    A   It takes ages to finish.

    B   It's got quite a confusing story.

    C   It's easier than others they've played.

12   You will hear a girl telling a friend about a hockey match she played in.
     What does she say about it?

    A   It was spoiled by the weather.

    B   The two teams weren't at the same level.

    C   There were problems with the playing area.

13   You will hear a boy telling a friend about a documentary he watched.
     What did he enjoy most about it?

    A   the soundtrack

    B   the interviews

    C   the location

Part 3

For each question, write the correct answer in the gap. Write **one** or **two words** or a **number** or a **date** or a **time**.

You will hear a radio announcement about a song-writing competition.

Competition: Write the words of a song

How to enter:

- click on the **(14)**..................... on the website

- complete the application form

- receive a **(15)**..................... by email

- listen to the sound file

What you hear:

- the tune played on a **(16)**.....................

What you have to do:

- write the words of the song

- choose a **(17)**..................... for it

Last date for entering:

- **(18)**.....................

First prize:

- **(19)**.....................

- hear your song on the radio

Questions 20 – 25

For each question, choose the correct answer.

You will hear an interview with a boy called Sam Wilson who collects film figurines, which are small plastic models of film characters.

20 What does Sam say about his grandfather's collection of postage stamps?

    A   He couldn't hide the fact that he found them boring.

    B   He didn't understand what he was told about them.

    C   He wasn't able to see the reason for having them.

21 Sam started his collection of figurines after

    A   receiving one as a gift.

    B   learning about them in art classes.

    C   a family member suggested the idea.

22 For Sam, the fun of collecting figurines comes from

    A   knowing how valuable they are.

    B   having a display of them at home.

    C   searching for pieces that are hard to find.

23 How does Sam decide which figurines he wants to collect?

    A   He wants to own all the characters from one film.

    B   He follows the example of other collectors.

    C   He chooses the more complicated ones.

24 Sam prefers to collect used figurines because

    A   he doesn't want to spend too much money.

    B   he likes to imagine where they came from.

    C   he thinks they will be easier to sell.

25 What does Sam say about his favourite figure?

    A   it's particularly well made

    B   lots of people have admired it

    C   he's very careful not to damage it

Part 1 (2–3 minutes)

Phase 1

- What's your name?
- How old are you?
- Where do you live?
- Who do you live with?

Phase 2

- Have you ever cooked a meal for family or friends? (Why?/Why not?)
- Do you like mornings or evenings best? (Why?)
- What's your favourite colour? (Why?)
- Do you enjoy winter sports? (Why?/Why not?)
- Do you often ride a bike? (Why?/Why not?)
- Would you like to play a musical instrument? (Why?/Why not?)
- Tell us about your family.
- Do you watch television in the evenings? (Why?/Why not?)

Part 2 (2–3 minutes)

5A Out walking

Now I'd like each of you to talk on your own about something.

I'm going to give each of you a photograph and I'd like you to talk about it.

A, here is your photograph. It shows **people out walking**.
[*Turn to photograph 5A on page 194.*]

B, you just listen.

A, please tell us what you can see in the photograph.

🕐 about 1 minute

Thank you.

5B Doing homework

B, here is your photograph.

It shows **someone doing homework**.

[*Turn to photograph 5B on page 198.*]

A, you just listen.

B, please tell us what you can see in the photograph.

🕐 about 1 minute

Thank you.

Part 3 (2–3 minutes)

Now, in this part of the test you're going to talk about something together for about two minutes. I'm going to describe a situation to you.

[*Turn to the task on page 204.*]

A girl has won an important race and her friends want to do something with her to celebrate. They all like sport.

Here are some things they could do with her.

Talk together about the things they could do to celebrate, and say which would be most fun.

All right? Now talk together.

 2–3 minutes

Thank you.

Part 4 (2–3 minutes)

- • Do you often celebrate things with friends? (Why?/Why not?)
- • Do you prefer to arrange to do activities with your friends or just hang out? (Why?)
- • Have you ever taken part in a sports competition? (Why?/Why not?)
- • Is it better to watch sports competitions or take part in them? (Why?)
- • Is it important for everyone to do sport? (Why?/Why not?)

 2–3 minutes

Thank you.

Part 1

Questions 1 – 5

For each question, choose the correct answer.

1

> ART STUDENTS
>
> At end of lesson, please return paints to cupboard, wash brushes and leave to dry by sink.

A Students should leave paints by the sink ready for the next lesson.

B Students should clean their brushes after they've finished using them.

C Students should wash all the equipment before putting it back in the cupboard.

2

< Back   Contacts

> Kate,
> I've looked everywhere for a present for Ramini but I can't afford anything in the jewellery shops you recommended. What else could I get her that she'll like?
> Asma

What is Asma asking Kate to do?

A go on a shopping trip to get a present for Ramini

B find out from Ramini what kind of present she'd like

C suggest another suitable gift for Ramini

3

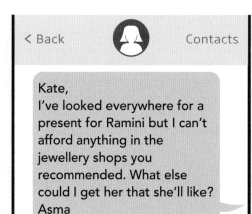

> We have stopped using plastic for our burger boxes – these are now made of recycled cardboard instead.

A The restaurant has started to use recycled cardboard due to customer demand.

B The restaurant will recycle the burger boxes when customers have finished with them.

C The restaurant has given up serving its burgers in plastic boxes.

4

New Message   — ⤢ ✕

To: All students   Cc   Bcc

From: Tour of football stadium

Spaces for this tour are still
available. We need a minimum
group size of 20 for the trip to
take place.

Sign up by this Friday.

Mrs Kingsley

Send

A   This visit might be cancelled if not enough people want to go on it.

B   There are only enough spaces for twenty people to take part in this trip.

C   Students have the chance to be shown around the stadium on Friday.

5

Judy phoned about the tennis
tournament. Could you let her
know if you have a spare racket?
Hers is broken, the shop's shut and
there's no time to fix it by her first
game tomorrow.

A   Judy would like help with repairing her racket tomorrow.

B   Judy wants information about the tournament starting tomorrow.

C   Judy needs to borrow a racket for a match she's playing tomorrow.

Part 2

For each question, choose the correct answer.

The young people below all want to join a club for people who enjoy reading.
On the opposite page there are descriptions of eight book clubs for teenagers.
Decide which club would be the most suitable for the people below.

6  Jenny wants a club where she can attend face-to-face meetings to discuss stories she's read. She also wants to get recommendations on novels she can read for free.

7  Eddy would like to join a club which organises talks by writers. He'd like the chance to buy cheap books on many subjects and to write book reviews.

8  Kasia loves reading about animals and wants a club where she can talk to people online who share her interest. She'd also like to practise her other favourite hobby, photography.

9  Joshua wants an online reading club where he can start his own blog about novels he's read. He's interested in fiction by people in his age group and wants to post his short stories.

10  Lilly loves reading but isn't interested in fiction. She wants a club which has special offers on books and also competitions.

Book clubs for teenagers

A   Library Club

Our members are book lovers who read and then recommend books that we should buy for the town library – from textbooks to novels and comics. We also meet after school at the library to help keep it tidy, and sometimes we pick which old books to give away to the public for free.

B   Book Wizards

Book Wizards recently won the title 'Book Club of the Year'. Members say club meetings are always friendly and enjoyable, and they have the opportunity to talk about books they've read. Often they're about subjects other than fiction, for example technology, animals or sport.

C   Book World

This web-based club is looking for members to run the Book World site, writing articles, taking and uploading pictures, and making sure information is up-to-date. The club has various chatrooms for discussing different types of books, from novels to wildlife or cooking.

D   Readers

Members of this friendly book club post reviews on the club web page of novels they've enjoyed. They get together once a month and exchange books – great if you don't want to have to buy new books – and share their opinions of different novels.

E   Love Books

This club is perfect for those who'd like to explore books about science, history, the natural world, and so on, rather than novels. There's an annual meeting, and four times a year, members receive a magazine which is full of reviews, cartoons and chances to win prizes. Members also receive money off at Harleys' bookstores.

F   Book Fans

This club for young people is run by the bookshop of the same name, and members get a generous fifty percent discount in all departments in the shop. Another club benefit is invitations to hear authors speak about their latest work for free. Members are also invited to post short articles on the club website about books they've read.

G   Read It

Members of this club chat online about different kinds of stories they've read, like science fiction, comedy and historical novels. The club's web pages are run by a publishing company and they're always good fun to look at, with videos and cartoons, and a monthly competition to win books.

H   Mad About Books

This is *the* club for book fans who want to share their opinions about literature, especially by teenage authors. Club members receive help in setting up their own web page on the site, where they can also upload their writing work and get feedback from other members and professional authors.

Questions 11 – 15

For each question, choose the correct answer.

Our class trip to the University's Media Studies department, by Flo Collins

One of the subjects at my school is called Media Studies. In the lessons, we learn about television, radio, film and video, newspapers, advertising and the computer games industry. As part of the course, our class recently visited a nearby university to meet Media Studies students there and do a project with them. After having a quick tour of the university, we were taken to the Media Studies department's TV studio. It was bigger than I expected, with rows of comfortable seats for the audience and amazing technology – just how I imagine a proper studio to be.

We took our seats and listened to three Media Studies staff describing what it's like to study the subject at university. A range of topics were discussed, including the contents of the course and future jobs. Some of us put questions that we'd thought of at school to the staff. I didn't get to ask my question, but I didn't mind as I wasn't keen to talk in front of such a large group of people.

Next, the university students organised a discussion about Media Studies topics. All of us in the audience were given the chance to vote on certain things, for example, 'In the future fewer people will watch TV. Do you agree?' It was very interesting to see that people shared so many opinions. After the discussion, we were divided into teams for our projects.

Each team had to create something to show to all the other teams at the end of the day. One group made a radio news report, another produced a sad documentary about rainforests, and another made a funny advert to promote a trip to Mars. My group started with some team-building exercises, before going on to write and practise performing a short drama about robots. For me, this experience made the whole day worth it. Everyone worked really hard and the results were fantastic. The day allowed me to try out something completely different and get an idea of how exciting it is to take Media Studies at university. Who knows, I might decide to continue with the subject when I go to university.

11 In the first paragraph, what does Flo say about visiting the university?

    A She regretted that the tour was so short.

    B She was surprised the university had a TV studio.

    C She was impressed by the facilities she saw.

    D She met some very helpful students there.

12 How did Flo feel during the 'Question and Answer' session?

    A uncomfortable about speaking in public

    B worried that her question would sound silly

    C disappointed that she wasn't chosen to speak

    D annoyed about forgetting to prepare a question

13 When the students were asked to vote, Flo noticed that

    A they weren't asked about very many topics.

    B there was a high level of agreement among them.

    C people decided not to vote on some subjects.

    D some of them had to think a lot about how to vote.

14 What is Flo doing in the final paragraph?

    A describing how the groups chose their projects

    B explaining how people reacted to her group's project

    C providing several examples of the group projects

    D saying why her group's project was the most interesting

15 What might Flo tell her parents about the Media Studies day?

    A I really enjoyed the Media Studies day, but it was a pity that some of the other students didn't work very hard on their projects.

    B Spending a day at the university has convinced me that I want to become a student there when I finish school.

    C I learnt so much from the Media Studies day, but the best thing about it was that I laughed from start to finish.

    D The Media Studies day was good fun, but I preferred the team activity best of all.

Part 4

Questions 16 – 20

Five sentences have been removed from the text below.

For each question, choose the correct answer.

There are three extra sentences which you do not need to use.

Old photos found in a suitcase

James Trenchard was twelve years old when he and his family moved house. The family's new home was a large house in London built in the 1800s. It had more space than they needed, including a spare bedroom. **16** [ ] The family didn't try to move it and they just filled the room with boxes of things they didn't have time to unpack.

After a few months, James went into the spare bedroom, looking for some of his old school books that were still in the boxes. **17** [ ] He pushed and pulled at the door without success. It seemed to be stuck, so James decided to make a bit more effort. **18** [ ] Inside was a large leather suitcase covered in dust.

James lifted it out of the wardrobe. It was very heavy and James was immediately curious about the contents. He got his dad to help him break the lock on the suitcase. **19** [ ] That was because inside there were hundreds and hundreds of amazing black and white photos, all of London in the 1930s. They showed people sitting on the roofs of buses, policemen in the middle of busy streets directing traffic, and even circus elephants walking along a road.

None of these were places in London that James recognised. **20** [ ] They didn't know what to do, so, after some discussion, father and son took the suitcase and its contents to a museum. The photos were looked at by staff there, who said this was one of the most important collections of photographs ever found. They are now appearing in an exhibition.

A   They weren't familiar to his dad either.

B   So he went downstairs and gave this key to his parents.

C   While searching for these, he wondered what was in the old wardrobe.

D   So they asked several experts what they should do.

E   He tried one last time, and suddenly it flew open.

F   This contained an ancient wardrobe left behind by the previous owner.

G   When they finally got it open, they couldn't believe their eyes.

H   They selected the best one hundred photos for public display.

Part 5

Questions 21 – 26

For each question, choose the correct answer.

The Gobi Desert

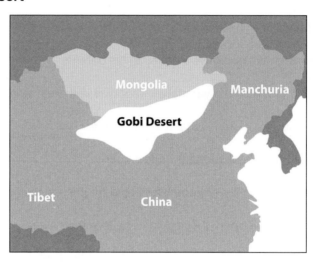

The Gobi Desert covers a huge area of Northern China and Southern Mongolia. The word *gobi* **(21)**.................. means 'very large and very dry' in the Mongolian language.

When we think of deserts, what often comes into our **(22)**.................. is a place with lots of sand, such as the Sahara Desert. However, most of the Gobi isn't like that at all. There are some areas of sand and mountains, but mostly the Gobi **(23)**.................. of flat rock. This means it is **(24)**.................. to drive across it for long distances.

The northwestern corner of the Gobi is **(25)**.................. for being somewhere where dinosaur bones can be found. Experts have **(26)**.................. a lot research here and dug up some truly exciting things. Although dinosaurs no longer live there, the Gobi Desert is home to bears, camels, wolves and many other wild animals.

21	**A**	specially	**B**	correctly	**C**	perfectly	**D**	actually
22	**A**	minds	**B**	attitudes	**C**	ideas	**D**	opinions
23	**A**	involves	**B**	consists	**C**	includes	**D**	contains
24	**A**	able	**B**	likely	**C**	possible	**D**	proper
25	**A**	particular	**B**	familiar	**C**	active	**D**	famous
26	**A**	made	**B**	taken	**C**	done	**D**	given

Questions 27 – 32

For each question, write the correct answer.

Write **one** word for each gap.

Playing in a band

Last year my older brother and his mates decided to start a band. I can play the
guitar so I asked **(27)**............... it was ok for me to be in their band, too. When they
refused to let me join, I decided to start a band of my **(28)**................. .

To find some other band members, I posted messages online and put up a
(29)............... posters round my school. Lots of people replied, saying there were
really interested **(30)**............... joining. It took weeks for me to meet them all and
choose my bandmates.

Anyway, **(31)**............... are now five of us in the band, and we've called ourselves
Plan D. We've practised loads and have entered a local competition called *Battle of
the Bands*. It's on next week and I can't wait to take **(32)**............... – my brother's
band are entering the competition too.

Part 1

You **must** answer this question.

Write your answer in about **100 words**.

Question 1

Read this email from your English-speaking friend Gina and the notes you have made.

New Message
From: Gina
Subject: Party for Ali

Ali's leaving to return to his home country next month. I'd like to organise a leaving party for him. ◄········ *Good idea!*

We could have a barbecue at my house, or we could go to the park for a picnic. Which is better? ◄········ *Explain*

I'd also like to buy Ali a leaving present. What present do you think he'd like? ◄········ *Suggest*

Let me know if you'd like to help organise the party. ◄········ *Say how you can help*

Part 2

Choose **one** of these questions.

Write your answer in about **100 words**.

Question 2

You see this announcement in your school English-language magazine.

> **Articles wanted!**
> **Enjoying Sport**
> Write an article telling us about a sport you do and why you enjoy it.
> How important do you think it is for teenagers to play sport? Why?
> The best articles answering these questions will be published next month.

Write your **article**.

Question 3

Your English teacher has asked you to write a story.

Your story must begin with this sentence.

Sam read the text message and felt worried.

Write your **story**.

Part 1

Questions 1 – 7

For each question, choose the correct answer.

1   What does the boy's sister do now?

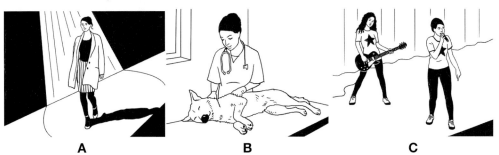

A   B   C

2   What has the girl bought for her room?

A   B   C

3   What did the boy buy at the stadium?

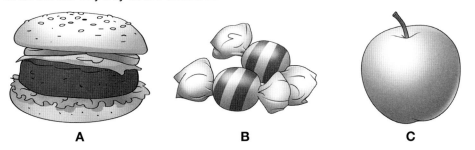

A   B   C

4   Which animal did the boy see a film about?

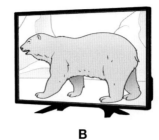

A   B   C

5   How much was the boy's jacket?

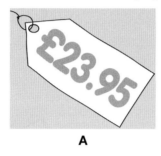

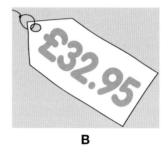

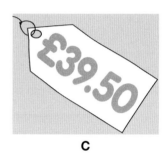

A   B   C

6   How is the family going on holiday?

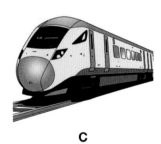

A   B   C

7   What did the girl leave at her friend's house?

A   B   C

Questions 8 – 13

For each question, choose the correct answer.

---

8 You will hear two friends talking about a day at the beach.
How did the girl feel about it?

- **A** impressed by the waves
- **B** disappointed with the weather
- **C** surprised at the number of people there

9 You will hear two students talking about their new maths teacher.
What did they both like about him?

- **A** He explained things very clearly.
- **B** He went through things slowly.
- **C** He made them laugh a lot.

10 You will hear a boy telling a friend about his room at home.
What is he doing?

- **A** explaining how he'd like to change it
- **B** describing how it looks at the moment
- **C** asking for suggestions for how to improve it

11 You will hear two friends talking about a sports quiz they took part in.
What did they think about it?

- **A** The questions were too hard.
- **B** The prizes weren't very interesting.
- **C** The other team wasn't very friendly.

12 You will hear two friends talking about a theme park they've been to.
How did the boy feel about the ride called 'Terror'?

- **A** worried how safe it was
- **B** unwell after being on it
- **C** keen to go on it again

13 You will hear two friends talking about a website they use.
What do they agree about it?

- **A** It's easy to find what you're looking for.
- **B** There are some useful graphics.
- **C** The videos are worth watching.

Part 3

Questions 14 – 19

For each question, write the correct answer in the gap. Write **one** or **two words** or a **number** or a **date** or a **time**.

___

You will hear a girl called Jessica giving a class presentation about a course she did for young people interested in becoming engineers.

Young engineer course

Minimum age for students: **(14)** ....

What you learn in the morning: **(15)** ....

What you have to bring: **(16)** ....

Piece of equipment that Jessica helped design: **(17)** ....

What all students are given at the end of the course: **(18)** ....

Website address for more information: www.**(19)** .... .com

Questions 20 – 25

For each question, choose the correct answer.

You will hear an interview with a boy called Aidan Gates, who's talking about being a member of his local Pony Association.

20   Aidan explains that the Pony Association's members

    A   are taught a range of skills connected to horses.

    B   join because they want to have riding lessons.

    C   all come from one particular age group.

21   Aidan first got involved in the association because

    A   a teacher recommended it.

    B   his parents knew somebody in it.

    C   one of his relatives introduced him to it.

22   Aidan explains that the Association uses horses which

    A   it buys from rich local families.

    B   are no longer wanted by their owners.

    C   wouldn't be ridden very much otherwise.

23   What does Aidan say about his school friends?

    A   They don't know what he does in his free time.

    B   They can't understand why horses are important to him.

    C   They're angry when he doesn't join in their social activities.

24   As a result of being in the association, Aidan has learnt

    A   why it's important to work hard.

    B   how new skills can change your life.

    C   that he's not interested in being the best.

25   How does Aidan feel about the presentation he's giving about the Association?

    A   confident that everything is ready

    B   nervous about making some mistakes

    C   worried about questions he'll be asked

Part 1 (2–3 minutes)

Phase 1

- What's your name?
- How old are you?
- Where do you live?
- Who do you live with?

Phase 2

- Do you ever read a newspaper? (Why?/Why not?)
- What do you usually eat for breakfast? (Why?)
- What type of films do you like? (Why?)
- Do you often go swimming? (Why?/Why not?)
- Do you enjoy watching sport? (Why?/Why not?)
- Do you enjoy shopping for clothes? (Why?/Why not?)
- Do you ever go running? (Why?/Why not?)
- Tell me about the place where you live.

Part 2 (2–3 minutes)

6A Time in town

Now I'd like each of you to talk on your own about something.

I'm going to give each of you a photograph and I'd like you to talk about it.

A, here is your photograph. It shows **friends spending time together in town**.

[*Turn to photograph 6A on page 194.*]

B, you just listen.

A, please tell us what you can see in the photograph.

about 1 minute

Thank you.

6B Eating at school

B, here is your photograph.

It shows **friends eating together at school**.

[*Turn to photograph 6B on page 198.*]

A, you just listen.

B, please tell us what you can see in the photograph.

about 1 minute

Thank you.

Part 3 (2–3 minutes)

Now, in this part of the test you're going to talk about something together for about two minutes. I'm going to describe a situation to you.

[*Turn to the task on page 205.*]

A brother and sister are going on a long bus journey, and want to take some things to pass the time. They only have a small bag with them.

Here are some things they could take.

Talk together about the different things they could take on the bus to pass the time and say which would be best.

All right? Now talk together.

🕐 2–3 minutes

Thank you.

Part 4 (2–3 minutes)

• Do you or your friends ever travel long distances by bus? (Why?/Why not?)
• What do you usually do to pass the time when you're travelling or waiting for something? (Why?)
• Do you think doing puzzles like crosswords is a good way to pass the time? (Why?/Why not?)
• Is it better to pass the time by doing something useful, or something fun? (Why?)
• Why do you think it's difficult to spend time waiting? (Why?/Why not?)

🕐 2–3 minutes

Thank you.

Part 1

Questions 1 – 5

For each question, choose the correct answer.

1

HOCKEY TEAM

No hockey practice today because school field is too wet and the sports hall is booked for badminton practice.

A Hockey practice today now has to take place indoors.

B Badminton practice will replace hockey practice today.

C Today's hockey practice is cancelled as there's nowhere for it to take place.

2

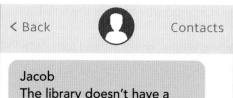

< Back   Contacts

Jacob
The library doesn't have a copy of the Geography book I need for the homework project. I guess I'll have to buy it. Can you let me know where you bought yours?
Alec

Why has Alec sent this text?

A To ask if Jacob wants to share the cost of buying a book.

B To find out how to get his own copy of the book.

C To check when Jacob borrowed the book from the library.

3

MICROWAVE POPCORN

Place bag correct side up in microwave.

Cook on full power 4 minutes.

Leave 2 minutes before serving.

A Be careful how you put the bag of popcorn in the microwave.

B Remove the bag of popcorn from the microwave after two minutes if it's cooked.

C Keep checking the bag of popcorn while it's in the microwave.

4

New Message   _ ↗ ×

To: Film club members   Cc   Bcc

As we've lost several members recently, can we all think about how we can increase membership and then discuss this at the next monthly meeting?

Kelly, Film club secretary

Send

Kelly wants to know

A   whether any other member would like to be club secretary.

B   what ideas people have for attracting new members to the club.

C   when club members are free to come to a meeting to discuss membership.

5

Ali

Arrived in Australia yesterday. The flight took absolutely ages, but we've been out today and visited an Australian wildlife park. Can't wait to see kangaroos in the wild. I'll send you some photos.

Peter

A   Peter has spent some of the day watching wild kangaroos in the countryside.

B   Peter's flight to Australia was very long so he hasn't done much today.

C   Peter is looking forward to seeing more animals during his trip to Australia.

Part 2

Questions 6 – 10

For each question, choose the correct answer.

The young people below all want to go on holiday with their family.

On the opposite page are descriptions of eight holiday companies offering holidays for families with teenagers.

Decide which holiday company would be the most suitable for the people below.

6  Marco wants to go on holiday with his parents and younger sister to somewhere really busy. They want a wide choice of places to eat out and don't want to stay in a hotel.

7  Katrin and her parents love doing watersports on holiday but they don't want to visit the sea. They've always stayed in hotels before, but now want something a bit different.

8  Shunsuke and his family are looking for a touring holiday that stops at many places. They enjoy art and history but don't like visiting busy attractions all the time.

9  Arjun and his father want a holiday where they can stay in two different places. Arjun enjoys outdoor activities, while his dad likes photographing landscapes.

10  Amy and her family enjoy active holidays that involve lots of challenges. They'd also like to see wildlife and they don't mind going somewhere hot.

Holidays for families with teenagers

A   Highland Holidays

Visit Scotland's capital and enjoy its culture, including world-famous museums and galleries, staying at a hotel or apartment in the heart of the city. Then continue your trip by coach through little-known towns and villages and learn about the country's past, staying at different traditional accommodation each night.

B   Weaver Travel

This is a great trip for families who love exploring wild places together. The conditions can sometimes get difficult as guests go off-road into the extreme heat of the jungle, but it's worth it when you discover monkeys, rare frogs and brightly-coloured birds. There are also chances to canoe in fast-flowing rivers and to go surfing.

C   Discovery Travel

Take your camera and good hiking boots, but pack light as this tour of Iceland moves on each night. There aren't many museums to visit here but the scenery is dramatic. The summer season is quite short compared to other places so it gets busy at some sights.

D   A–Z Trips

This camping trip is perfect for those who want to enjoy African animals in the wild, such as lions, rhinos, elephants and giraffes. Guests stay in tents in the Etosha National Park but camp assistants do everything for them, including cooking three delicious meals a day.

E   Jackson Holidays

Booking an apartment in a downtown location is cheaper than you might think and is the perfect way to make the most of lively cities that never go to sleep. Cultural attractions like museums and galleries, a huge variety of cheap places to get dinner and fantastic shopping are all within minutes of your door.

F   Island Holidays

This is a great place to spend your holiday if you love surfing or swimming in the sea. There are views of the Welsh mountains from the five-star hotel, which has an award-winning restaurant and an entertainment programme for all the family. There's also a choice of several excellent places to eat nearby.

G   Family Trips

This holiday starts in the mountains, with amazing views of icy lakes and snow-covered peaks. A camera is essential on this trip, but for younger or more adventurous guests there's snowboarding, snowshoe walking and skiing. Guests then transfer by luxury train to the lively city of Vancouver, where they stay at the finest hotel in town.

H   Footsteps Travel

This luxury camping holiday in the middle of the peaceful Irish countryside is perfect for those who want comfortable beds and a proper cooker to make meals on. The site is next to a lake where daily or weekly waterskiing and sailing lessons can be booked.

Questions 11 – 15

For each question, choose the correct answer.

My school 100 years ago by Jess Eames

Above the entrance to my school is a stone on which the date 1900 is written. I've often wondered what the school was like when it opened and how different it was for the students then. Recently I decided I just had to find some answers to my questions. My history teacher didn't know about the school's early history and suggested I try the local history section of the public library. I didn't know there was a section for that in the library and was amazed to find dozens of titles, including ones with old photos of my school.

I borrowed as many books as I was allowed. The first one I looked at contained a photo of a class of students and their teacher at my school. There was nothing about it I recognised except the school logo above a blackboard on which there were sums. There were about fifty students, with different year groups all mixed together. No one was smiling, but I read that was common in photos then.

Turning the pages of the other books, it was incredible to see so many photos. Children sat in long rows with nothing in front of them except a textbook and small board for doing sums or spelling tests on. The teachers were mainly women and only in their twenties. I later learnt that was because when a female teacher got married, she generally gave up her job. And everyone was dressed in smart clothes.

From my reading, I learnt loads more. Now I'm thinking about whether to write a report for the school newspaper or ask to give a talk to my classmates. Anyway, this all made me realise I'm really lucky I wasn't at school in those days. I know children had more holidays, but that was because they had to work in the fields. And they probably didn't get as good an education as us. Most kids left school before the age of twelve. Not only that, but school wasn't a healthy place to be in winter, as the classrooms were probably freezing. Only those in the front row benefited from the small heater beside the teacher's desk.

11 When Jess started researching her school, she was

    A convinced she would learn a lot of things.

    B disappointed there were so few books about local history.

    C surprised that so few people knew much about it.

    D curious to know how school life today compared with the past.

12 When Jess looked at the photo in the first book

    A she thought it was taken at a different school.

    B she realised how strict teachers were then.

    C she noticed there were students of various ages in the class.

    D she decided the lessons looked very boring.

13 What does Jess say about the school photos she found in other books?

    A Most of the teachers looked quite young.

    B The seats seemed to be uncomfortable.

    C The students had nothing to write on.

    D The children's clothes were torn.

14 What is Jess doing in the final paragraph?

    A Arguing for changes to the length of the school day.

    B Explaining why she's grateful to be a student now.

    C Describing what people did to improve the school.

    D Suggesting that schools copy the old teaching methods.

15 What might Jess say about researching the history of her school?

    A

> I really enjoyed learning about education in 1900, especially because I found out things that my history teacher didn't know.

    B

> Finding out about my school was easy because so much has been written about it, but I wish I had found more photos.

    C

> It was really interesting to do this independent research, but I haven't decided if I'm going to tell others about what I discovered.

    D

> My history teacher enjoyed my report so much that he's now asked the whole class to do a project on this topic during lessons.

Part 4

Five sentences have been removed from the text below.

For each question, choose the correct answer.

There are three extra sentences which you do not need to use.

Alexander Selkirk – the real Robinson Crusoe

Alexander Selkirk was a sailor who had many adventures, including living alone on an island in the South Pacific Ocean. Many people believe the novel called *Robinson Crusoe* was based on Alexander's life.

Alexander Selkirk's real family name was Selcraig. He was born in a Scottish fishing village in 1676 and was known throughout the village for his bad behaviour. After getting into a fight with his brothers, he was told to appear before a court of law. **16** [ ] Changing his surname to Selkirk, he left Scotland to take part in an expedition to South America. However, this wasn't an ordinary trip at all: Alexander had joined a pirate ship.

Life on board the ship was tougher than nineteen-year-old Alexander had imagined. **17** [ ] This led to anger and disagreements among the crew. What made the situation worse was that the ship's captain, Charles Pickering, became ill with a fever, and an officer called Thomas Stradling took control of the ship. **18** [ ] Both Thomas Stradling and Alexander Selkirk were young, proud and had strong characters. Their dislike of each other increased while the ship stopped at an unknown island in the South Pacific.

When it was time for the ship to continue its journey, Alexander refused to go, insisting the ship wasn't safe. **19** [ ] He was sure the rest of the crew would agree with him and not with the captain, but he was wrong. However, Alexander was convinced it was dangerous to stay on the ship so he demanded that they leave him on the island. Unfortunately for him, the ship sailed off and left him alone there with hardly any food.

Alexander had to live all by himself until he was rescued four years later by another passing ship. During his time on the island, he hunted for lobster and other shellfish. **20** [ ] He kept himself busy building fires and a hut to live in, but he was always lonely. When Alexander was finally rescued, he learnt that Thomas Stradling's ship had been unsafe and had sunk.

A   This new captain was extremely unpopular, and fights became common.

B   He also collected wild fruit and vegetables to eat.

C   Alexander regretted his decision to leave the island.

D   The sailors had little to eat and suffered many illnesses.

E   The two of them had nothing in common.

F   To support his argument, he pointed out all the repairs it needed.

G   His family never stopped worrying about him.

H   To avoid being punished, he decided to run away.

Part 5

Questions 21 – 26

For each question, choose the correct answer.

The Golden Gate Bridge

The Golden Gate Bridge in San Francisco, USA, was built between 1933 and 1937. The idea for building the bridge was first suggested back in 1872, but at that time the project was felt to be impossible. Finally, in 1924, the decision was **(21)**................. to build the bridge. When it first opened, it was the longest bridge of its **(22)**............... in the world.

The bridge **(23)**.................. the San Francisco bay and is 2.7 kilometres long. It is 27 metres wide and its towers **(24)**.................. 227 metres above the water. The other thing you notice about the bridge is that it's painted orange, or 'international orange' to be **(25)**.................. .

Today, the bridge is one of the **(26)**.................. tourist attractions in San Francisco and is known all over the world.

21	**A**	set	**B**	made	**C**	got	**D**	brought
22	**A**	way	**B**	method	**C**	fashion	**D**	kind
23	**A**	crosses	**B**	covers	**C**	cuts	**D**	continues
24	**A**	develop	**B**	carry	**C**	grow	**D**	rise
25	**A**	right	**B**	proper	**C**	exact	**D**	direct
26	**A**	total	**B**	main	**C**	certain	**D**	strong

Questions 27 – 32

For each question, write the correct answer.

Write **one** word for each gap.

My visit to Liverpool football stadium by Joachim Hantelmann

Last summer my family and I travelled from Germany to the UK. We went there to visit my mum's cousin **(27)**................. now lives in Liverpool.

It was our first time in the city so we decided to **(28)**................. sightseeing, starting with the famous Liverpool Football stadium at Anfield. The tickets were less expensive than I expected. **(29)**................. are tours of the stadium almost every day during summer, and these are offered **(30)**................. nine languages. My mum said we had to do the English-speaking tour because it was useful language practice for us.

The tour was amazing. We saw the dressing rooms **(31)**................. the teams get changed, and we sat in the players' box beside the pitch. The best part of the whole tour was when we ran out onto the pitch just **(32)**................. the players do at the start of a game.

Part 1

You **must** answer this question.

Write your answer in about **100 words**.

Question 1

Read this email from your English friend Morgan and the notes you have made.

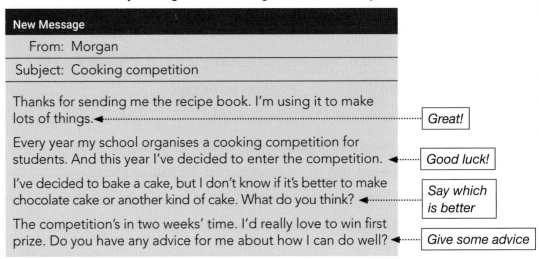

New Message
From: Morgan
Subject: Cooking competition

Thanks for sending me the recipe book. I'm using it to make lots of things. ◄·········· *Great!*

Every year my school organises a cooking competition for students. And this year I've decided to enter the competition. ◄········ *Good luck!*

I've decided to bake a cake, but I don't know if it's better to make chocolate cake or another kind of cake. What do you think? ◄············ *Say which is better*

The competition's in two weeks' time. I'd really love to win first prize. Do you have any advice for me about how I can do well? ◄······· *Give some advice*

Write your **email** to Morgan using **all the notes**.

Part 2

Choose **one** of these questions.

Write your answer in about **100 words**.

Question 2

You see this announcement in your school English-language magazine.

Articles wanted!
SHOPPING
What do you and your friends like to buy when you go shopping?
Do you think shopping is a good way for young people to spend their free time?
The best articles answering these questions will be published next month.

Write your **article**.

Question 3

Your English teacher has asked you to write a story.

Your story must begin with this sentence.

Just as my friend and I were leaving the museum, the alarm bell started ringing.

Write your **story**.

Questions 1 – 7

For each question, choose the correct answer.

---

1   What did the boy take photos of?

      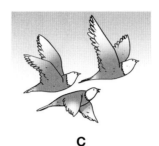

     A   **B**   **C**

2   What will they have for lunch?

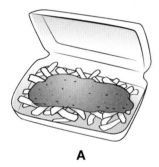   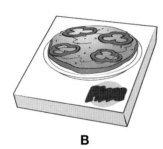   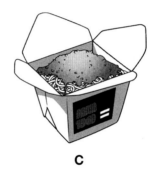

     A   **B**   **C**

3   What is the discount for school students on Mondays?

Student Discount ★ **10%** ★	Student Discount ★ **15%** ★	Student Discount ★ **20%** ★
A	**B**	**C**

4   Which rucksack does the girl choose?

A   B   C

5   What did the girl draw in her art class?

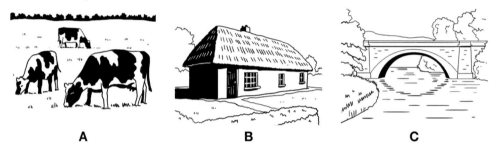

A   B   C

6   Why was the football match cancelled?

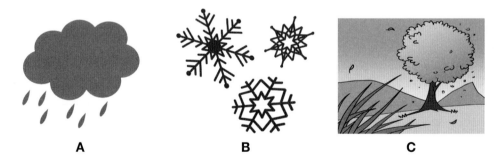

A   B   C

7   What will the girl do this weekend?

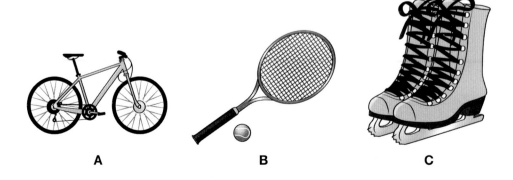

A   B   C

Part 2

Questions 8 – 13

For each question, choose the correct answer.

---

8   You will hear a girl telling a friend about her trip to Canada.
    How did she feel before she started the trip?

    A   concerned about flying alone

    B   worried about her language skills

    C   unsure if she was prepared for the weather

9   You will hear two friends talking about performing in a school concert.
    What do they agree was the hardest part?

    A   knowing who was in the audience

    B   finding the time to do enough practice

    C   remembering what they'd been told to do

10   You will hear two friends talking about homework.
    What does the girl advise the boy to do?

    A   a search on the internet

    B   compare notes with a classmate

    C   ask someone to suggest a website

11   You will hear two friends talking about a collection of short stories.
    What is the boy doing?

    A   explaining why he's enjoyed reading it

    B   comparing it with another similar book

    C   suggesting who the writer might be

12   You will hear two friends talking about a dance club.
    What does the girl think about it?

    A   the music is rather uninteresting

    B   the building needs cleaning

    C   the teacher is quite strict

13   You will hear two friends talking about a statue.
    What does the girl like about it?

    A   what it looks like

    B   what it's made from

    C   what it reminds her of

Part 3

Questions 14 – 19

For each question, write the correct answer in the gap. Write **one** or **two words** or a **number** or a **date** or a **time**.

You will hear a teenage footballer called Selma talking about a football summer camp which has special training for goalkeepers.

Goalkeeper training

Selma's **(14)**.................... helped her find the football summer camp.

Selma enjoyed practising her **(15)**.................... skills with the whole group of players.

The specific training for goalkeepers started at **(16)**.................... o'clock in the morning.

Selma says she needed to practise **(17)**.................... skills for her goalkeeping.

Selma thinks that goalkeepers should always wear **(18)**.................... as part of their kit.

The company which runs the training is called **(19)**.................... Training.

Questions 20 – 25

For each question, choose the correct answer.

You will hear an interview with a young singer-songwriter called Marcus Bushel.

20   Marcus says that as a young child

    A   he preferred playing the piano to singing.

    B   he didn't like the idea of performing in public.

    C   he had lots of friends who shared his interests.

21   Marcus thinks he won the school talent competition because

    A   he was an experienced songwriter.

    B   he thought about what he was singing.

    C   he was able to play his own instrument.

22   What does Marcus say about his training as a singer?

    A   He missed lessons in other subjects to do it.

    B   He was shown the mistakes that he was making.

    C   He learnt how to make the most of his natural ability.

23   Marcus prefers not to sing in a band because

    A   he thinks it doesn't suit his character.

    B   he dislikes the type of music they play.

    C   he isn't keen on working with other people.

24   Marcus says that the singer Steffi Phlox is going to

    A   promote him as a recording artist.

    B   put him in touch with a recording studio.

    C   sing some of his songs on her next album.

25   Marcus would advise talented young musicians

    A   to put their general education first.

    B   to make every effort to make it their career.

    C   to accept that they're unlikely to be successful.

Part 1 (2–3 minutes)

Phase 1

- What's your name?
- How old are you?
- Where do you live?
- Who do you live with?

Phase 2

- How do you travel home from school every day? (Why?)
- What subjects do you enjoy most at school? (Why?)
- What type of music do you enjoy? (Why?)
- Tell us about something you did yesterday.
- Do you enjoy the same types of film as your friends? (Why?/Why not?)
- Do you ever go to museums? (Why?/Why not?)
- Do you watch the news on television? (Why?/Why not?)
- Tell us about the house or apartment where you live.

Part 2 (2–3 minutes)

7A Eating at home

Now I'd like each of you to talk on your own about something.

I'm going to give each of you a photograph and I'd like you to talk about it.

A, here is your photograph. It shows **people eating at home**.

[*Turn to photograph 7A on page 195.*]

B, you just listen.

A, please tell us what you can see in the photograph.

🕐 about 1 minute

Thank you.

7B People on holiday

B, here is your photograph. It shows **people on holiday**.

[*Turn to photograph 7B on page 199.*]

A, you just listen.

B, please tell us what you can see in the photograph.

🕐 about 1 minute

Thank you.

Part 3 (2–3 minutes)

Now, in this part of the test you're going to talk about something together for about two minutes. I'm going to describe a situation to you.

[*Turn to the task on page 206.*]

A school wants students to do an interesting activity on the last day of the school year.

Here are some activities the students could do.

Talk together about the different activities the students could do, and say which would be most interesting for all the students.

All right? Now talk together.

 2–3 minutes

Thank you.

Part 4 (2–3 minutes)

- What happens on the last day of the school year in your school?
- What do you do with friends at school in breaks between lessons? (Why?)
- Do you think the school holidays are long enough? (Why?/Why not?)
- Should students have to do homework in the school holidays? (Why?/Why not?)
- What's the best thing about being at school? (Why?)

 2–3 minutes

Thank you.

Part 1

Questions 1 – 5

For each question, choose the correct answer.

1

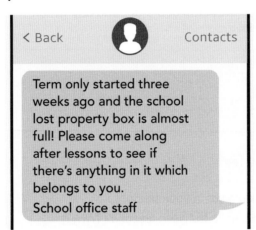

The school office staff

A have lost something and need help finding it.

B would like students to take the items they've lost.

C are asking people to be careful not to lose their things.

2

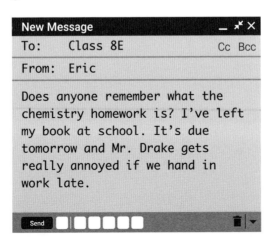

A You can get the latest books at a special price at the moment.

B You will only be able to buy the older books for a while longer.

C You should request the most recent books now to get them in time.

3

New Message

To: Class 8E   Cc Bcc

From: Eric

Does anyone remember what the chemistry homework is? I've left my book at school. It's due tomorrow and Mr. Drake gets really annoyed if we hand in work late.

Send

Why is Eric writing to his classmates?

A to remind them to do their homework

B to ask them what he has to do for homework

C to find out who has taken his homework book

4

Can you answer the question below? Text now! Free cinema tickets for the first ten people to send in the correct answer.

You'll only get a prize if

A you send the right answer quickly enough.

B you've bought the right type of ticket.

C you text the right answers to ten questions.

5

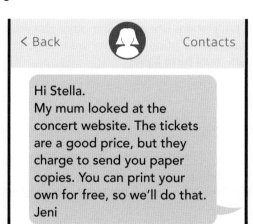

< Back   Contacts

Hi Stella.
My mum looked at the concert website. The tickets are a good price, but they charge to send you paper copies. You can print your own for free, so we'll do that.
Jeni

A Jeni is suggesting a way to make it cheaper to see the concert.

B Jeni is telling Stella they'll have to pay more than they expected.

C Jeni is explaining why they should buy the tickets from a different website.

Questions 6 – 10

For each question, choose the correct answer.

The young people below are all looking for a park to go to at the weekend.

On the opposite page there are descriptions of eight parks.

Decide which park would be the most suitable for the people below.

6  Celine wants to go to a park which doesn't get too busy. She needs to be able to get there on public transport and would like to learn about the animals and trees there.

7  Samir and his friends are looking for a park with an area for skateboarders, and where they can buy refreshments. Samir's father is taking them, so he'll need somewhere to leave his car.

8  Paulina is looking for a park where she and her mother can walk their dog. They'd like it to have a wood, and they want to go in the evenings, so the park must have lights.

9  Max and his family are looking for a park which has a playground, lots of room for a game of football and somewhere for a barbecue.

10  Liza is looking for a park that has an exercise class she can join, and somewhere to have a swim afterwards. She also wants a safe place to leave her bike.

Parks

A Hybury Park

Hybury Park has huge open fields, a wood and an area for cooking over fires. If you prefer to buy your food, there's a shop, with space outside for bikes. There's also a car park and a children's area with a slide, a roundabout and trees to climb. The park closes at 5 p.m.

B Trentam Park

This pretty park has notices giving information on the wildlife and plants you might see there. It's hidden away behind a station, so not many people know about it, which is a pity as it has a lovely playground and a café with space outside for locking up bikes.

C Oaklands Park

This is a popular park, especially with those who enjoy wildlife, so the car park is often full. There's a skate park and some exercise machines next to the children's play area, which is safer now as dog walking is no longer permitted. Several bus routes pass nearby and the park has street lights.

D Fenton Park

Fenton Park has a skate park and plenty of open spaces with few trees, so it's good for walking dogs or doing exercise, but there's no car park. It's a fun place to spend time as there's a barbecue area and a café. And with the lights along the paths, you won't get lost after dark.

E Gatston Park

Gatston Park isn't easy to travel to by bus, but there's a car park and a little hut where you can lock up bicycles. There are lots of woodland creatures around, and everyone loves the pool. In the evenings you'll often see a fitness group for teenagers with an instructor.

F Somers Park

Somers Park has a café, playground and football fields, but most people go for the skate park. It can get busy, so if you prefer to avoid crowds, try early mornings or late evenings. There isn't a car park, but there's plenty of space to park in the nearby streets.

G Newfields Park

This park is well-known for its outside pool and café, but there's a lot more you can do there, such as taking a walk with a guide to learn about the birds or using the outdoor exercise machines. There's also a picnic area and a large field where you can play games.

H Lakeside Park

There's plenty of space at Lakeside Park for skateboarders, dog walkers, runners and family groups. There's a lake, a small forest and a playground too. The park is well used right through until after dark, when the street lamps come on along the paths.

Part 3

For each question, choose the correct answer.

A short story competition

My name's Amy Shaw and I'm 13 years old. Recently I wrote a short story for a competition. I love writing, but I usually keep my stories to myself. But when my mum read about this national competition for teenagers, she said I should take part before it was too late – you have to be under 14 to enter. I'm so glad she did. I started immediately. I wrote a plan quite quickly, then used that to write the story. I spent ages changing things and rewriting until I was happy, then I sent it in. I read later that 50 000 people entered.

Six weeks later, Mum showed me an email she'd got. It said the judges had selected my story for the final. It was going to be at a museum, with a famous person reading each story. Mum said that, to attend, I'd have to miss a day of school and get a nice dress. I'm not great at choosing clothes, so I thought that might be a problem. Luckily, Mum helped me.

The day of the final was fantastic. I'll never forget it. Mum and Dad came with me to the museum, which was full of people. The ten finalists had to go up on the stage. Because we were all together, it was actually fun, rather than scary. The thing I remember most is listening to the actor reading my story. I enjoy acting at school, but I'll never be that good. For each character, he spoke in a different, often silly way, and made everyone laugh. My words sounded so much better the way he read them. We chatted afterwards, and he asked about what I'm writing now. I told him I've got lots of ideas.

My story didn't win, but I still got a prize; 40 books for me and 500 for my school. There was hardly space for them all in the library! The head teacher asked me to stand up in front of the whole school and explain how I'd won them. I was a bit embarrassed, but it's great to have won a prize that everyone can get some benefit from.

11 What does Amy do in the first paragraph?

    A Encourage other people to write stories for competitions.

    B Tell people how to find out about writing competitions.

    C Complain about the rules of the competition.

    D Explain why she entered the competition.

12 How did Amy feel when she found out she was in the final?

    A Surprised that the judges liked her work.

    B Excited about meeting famous people.

    C Worried about what she would wear.

    D Pleased about missing school.

13 Amy says that the actor who read her story

    A chatted with each of the competition finalists.

    B improved the story by using amusing voices.

    C made her consider becoming an actor.

    D gave her ideas for another story.

14 What does Amy say about the books that she won?

    A She feels proud to see them in her school.

    B She wishes there were not so many of them.

    C She is glad she can share them with her schoolmates.

    D She thinks they're better than what the winner received.

15 What would Amy write in her diary after the final?

    A It took me so long to write that story, but it was worth every minute.

    B I had the best day ever. It's just a shame that my family couldn't be there.

    C It's incredible to think that my story was the best one out of so many thousands.

    D There were so many people at the museum. I felt really nervous.

Part 4

Questions 16 – 20

Five sentences have been removed from the text below.

For each question, choose the correct answer.

There are three extra sentences which you do not need to use.

The problem of insects in museums

Most of us have spent time at a museum, perhaps on a school trip, looking at and learning about the things on display. But how many of us have ever thought about how these objects are kept in good condition? **16** [ ] They make sure the temperature and light levels are always just right, and that the air isn't too humid.

However, even if the conditions are correct, there are still things that can seriously damage a valuable object – insects. Often these enter the museum inside the object itself. **17** [ ] Once inside the museum, they can quickly move from one object to another, and particularly enjoy eating natural materials such as wood, cotton, silk and wool.

Museum experts say that the older the objects, the more the insects seem to be attracted to them. **18** [ ] People may no longer know the techniques or have the materials required to mend them. As a result, museums will try almost anything to prevent insects from damaging their collections. For example, a new object will be kept separately at first. Then, when staff are sure there are no insects inside, it can be put on display with everything else. If insects are found in a piece of clothing or art, placing it in a freezer is one way of getting rid of them.

But now one museum in the USA has decided to try something new. **19** [ ] Dogs have an excellent sense of smell, and are often taught to use this to help humans look for things. Usually the dog sits down to show that it has found what it's looking for. Staff at the Boston Museum of Fine Arts hope that their dog, Riley, will learn to do this when it finds insects. **20** [ ] However, if Riley can help find insects before they do much damage, other museums are sure to be interested.

A   That's a problem because these things can't easily be repaired.

B   That's why insects are the most important things to check for.

C   This is something museums put a lot of money and effort into.

D   Unfortunately, museums are no longer allowed to use these methods.

E   They say that at the moment it's just an experiment.

F   It's hoped this will attract more visitors, not more insects.

G   They may also by brought in by accident on visitors' clothes.

H   They are training a puppy to find insects.

Part 5

Questions 21 – 26

For each question, choose the correct answer.

Footgolf

Footgolf is a sport which has become quite popular in recent years. The first footgolf world cup competition was **(21)**.................. in Hungary in 2012, with just eight countries taking part. Four years later, 26 countries entered.

As its name **(22)**.................., footgolf is a mix of football and golf. Players move around a course, kicking a football from one hole to the next. The **(23)**.................. between the holes is shorter than in golf, because you can't kick a football as far as you can hit a golf ball. However, the game is similar to golf, as the **(24)**.................. is to get your ball into each hole using as few kicks as possible.

Footgolf can be played on golf courses, but with a different route and holes. However, it's best to play it on courses **(25)**.................. built for the sport. One reason footgolf is popular is that it doesn't require much **(26)**.................., so it's quite cheap to play.

21	**A**	done	**B**	kept	**C**	held	**D**	set
22	**A**	points	**B**	tells	**C**	advises	**D**	suggests
23	**A**	length	**B**	distance	**C**	limit	**D**	difference
24	**A**	reason	**B**	plan	**C**	aim	**D**	design
25	**A**	specially	**B**	exactly	**C**	completely	**D**	properly
26	**A**	baggage	**B**	equipment	**C**	property	**D**	contents

Questions 27 – 32

For each question, write the correct answer.

Write **one** word for each gap.

The school skiing trip by Molly Green, Class 9B

Last week, a group of students from my school went on a skiing trip. We travelled
to the mountains by coach. I wasn't looking **(27)**............... to the journey, but
actually it was fine. I was **(28)**............... busy chatting that I forgot I usually feel ill on
long journeys!

We were away for four days, and skied every day. We were divided into groups
depending **(29)**............... our level – I was in the beginners' group. Our teacher was
great. On the first morning, **(30)**............... of us could even stand up on our skis,
but after just a few hours we were all happily skiing down the less steep parts of
the mountain.

Everyone met up in the evenings for dinner, and we had fun telling **(31)**...............
other about our experiences.

If you enjoy skiing, or even if you've never skied before, maybe you should sign
(32)............... for next year's trip. I loved it!

Part 1

You **must** answer this question.

Write your answer in about **100 words**.

Question 1

Read the email from your English-speaking friend Kelly, and the notes you have made.

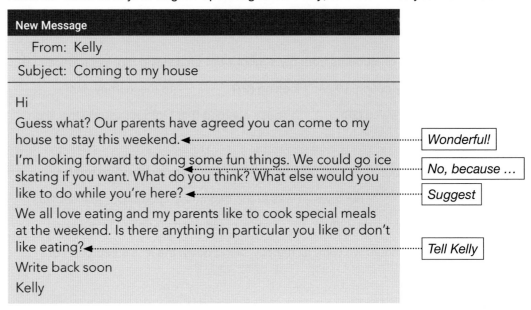

New Message
From: Kelly
Subject: Coming to my house

Hi

Guess what? Our parents have agreed you can come to my house to stay this weekend. ◄········· *Wonderful!*

I'm looking forward to doing some fun things. We could go ice skating if you want. What do you think? ◄ *No, because …*

What else would you like to do while you're here? ◄········· *Suggest*

We all love eating and my parents like to cook special meals at the weekend. Is there anything in particular you like or don't like eating? ◄········· *Tell Kelly*

Write back soon

Kelly

Write your **email** to Kelly using **all the notes**.

Part 2

Choose **one** of these questions.

Write your answer in about **100 words**.

Question 2

You see this announcement on an English-language website.

> **Homework**
> We'd like to publish articles by students about homework. Why do teachers want their students to do homework? Do students get too much homework? Should students have longer school days instead of doing homework?
> Write an article answering these questions. We'll publish the best ones on our website.

Write your **article**.

Question 3

Your English teacher has asked you to write a story.

Your story must begin with this sentence:

Abigail looked at her watch, then suddenly put her coat on and rushed out of the house.

Write your **story**.

Part 1

Questions 1 – 7

For each question, choose the correct answer.

1   What time does the film begin?

A   B   C

2   Which room should the students go to after the break?

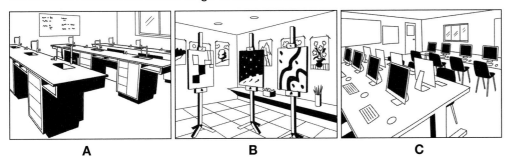

A   B   C

3   Which sport does the girl's brother play now?

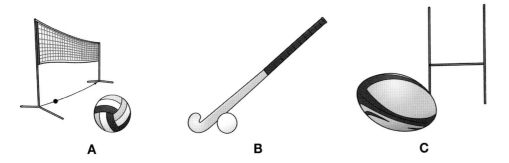

A   B   C

4 Which game did the boy like most?

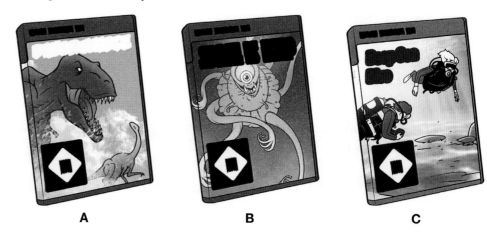

A   B   C

5 Where did the family stay on holiday?

A   B   C

6 What flavour ice cream does the boy choose?

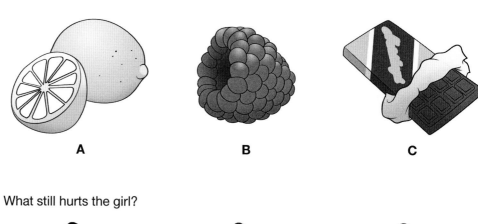

A   B   C

7 What still hurts the girl?

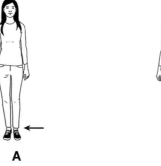 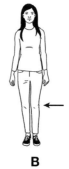 

A   B   C

Questions 8 – 13

For each question, choose the correct answer.

---

8   You will hear a girl telling a friend about a class presentation she has to do.
What is she worrying about?

    A   holding people's interest

    B   forgetting what comes next

    C   using a piece of technology

9   You will hear two friends talking about the village where they live.
What do they both think the village needs more of?

    A   sports facilities

    B   seats for the elderly

    C   children's play areas

10   You will hear a brother and sister talking about a birthday party.
What does the boy agree to do?

    A   organise the entertainments

    B   prepare the refreshments

    C   send out the invitations

11   You will hear two friends talking about a new shopping centre.
What do they agree about it?

    A   The range of shops is good.

    B   The places to eat look interesting.

    C   The transport links are convenient.

12   You will hear a girl telling a friend about changes at her school.
What is she doing?

    A   explaining the reasons for them

    B   suggesting some alternatives to them

    C   complaining about how they'll affect her

13   You will hear two friends talking about a museum visit.
What is the purpose of the visit?

    A   to see one object in particular

    B   to watch one very interesting video

    C   to take notes about one period of history

Questions 14 – 19

For each question, write the correct answer in the gap. Write **one** or **two words** or a **number** or a **date** or a **time**.

You will hear a boy called Simon giving a class presentation about a course in digital art he went on.

Course in Digital Art

The course costs **(14)** £................... for students who are still at school.

On the first day, students should bring a **(15)**................... with them.

Simon enjoyed the session on how to use **(16)**................... in digital artwork.

It's easy for students to **(17)**................... their work at home.

Simon's artwork can be seen in a **(18)**................... on the college website.

To find out about the course, send an email to **(19)**...................@college.com.

Questions 20 – 25

For each question, choose the correct answer.

You will hear an interview with a young breakdancer called Chelsea Fordham, who appears on music videos.

20 Why did Chelsea decide to take up breakdancing?

    A   She was impressed by some dancers she saw.

    B   Dancing used skills she'd learnt doing sports.

    C   Her family always wanted her to dance.

21 How did Chelsea learn breakdancing?

    A   She went on a course.

    B   She got some advice online.

    C   She watched what the experts did.

22 When she's creating a new dance routine, Chelsea likes to

    A   plan how long it's going to take.

    B   get to know the piece of music first.

    C   discuss her ideas with other people.

23 The type of singers that Chelsea enjoys making videos with

    A   have a relaxed attitude to their work.

    B   come up with good ideas on the day of filming.

    C   know what's expected of them and follow instructions.

24 When she works with her 'crew', Chelsea's role is to

    A   take the lead in performances.

    B   provide them with ideas and support.

    C   encourage them to try a range of styles.

25 What are Chelsea's plans for the immediate future?

    A   She's hoping to have a career in films.

    B   She's doing some work with a famous singer.

    C   She's thinking of starting a school for young dancers.

Part 1 (2–3 minutes)

Phase 1

- • What's your name?
- • How old are you?
- • Where do you live?
- • Who do you live with?

Phase 2

- • Do you usually travel to school with your friends? (Why?/Why not?)
- • What do you usually eat for lunch? (Why?)
- • What are you going to do tomorrow? (Why?)
- • Where would you like to go on your next holiday? (Why?)
- • Do you play any sports? (Why?/Why not?)
- • How often do you watch television? (Why?)
- • What do you use a mobile phone for?
- • What did you do on your last birthday?

Part 2 (2–3 minutes)

8A Meeting in town

Now I'd like each of you to talk on your own about something.

I'm going to give each of you a photograph and I'd like you to talk about it.

A, here is your photograph. It shows **friends meeting in town**.

[*Turn to photograph 8A on page 195.*]

B, you just listen.

A, please tell us what you can see in the photograph.

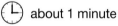 about 1 minute

Thank you.

8B Having a lesson

B, here is your photograph. It shows **people having a lesson**.

[*Turn to photograph 8B on page 199.*]

A, you just listen.

B, please tell us what you can see in the photograph.

 about 1 minute

Thank you.

Part 3 (2–3 minutes)

Now, in this part of the test you're going to talk about something together for about two minutes. I'm going to describe a situation to you.

[*Turn to the task on page 207.*]

A computer games shop wants more teenagers to go shopping there. They decide to give a free gift to teenage customers on their first visit.

Here are some of the gifts the shop could give.

Talk together about the different gifts the shop could give and say which would be most popular with teenagers.

All right? Now talk together.

 2–3 minutes

Thank you.

Part 4 (2–3 minutes)

• Has a shop ever given you a free gift? (Did you like it?)
• Do you think computer games are fun to play? (Why?/Why not?)
• What's your favourite type of shop? (Why?)
• Do you prefer going shopping with family, friends, or alone? (Why?)
• Do you think it's a good idea to buy things online? (Why?/Why not?)

 2–3 minutes

Thank you.

GRAMMAR BANK

Present simple

Positive

I/We/You/They	know.
He/She/It	know**s**.

Negative

I/We/You/They	**don't** know.
He/She/It	**doesn't** know.

Questions

Do	I/we/you/they	know?
Does	he/she/it	

Short answers

Yes,	I/we/you/they	**do**.
	he/she/it	**does**.
No,	I/we/you/they	**don't**.
	he/she/it	**doesn't**.

We use the present simple to talk about:

* permanent states.
  *He **lives** in Canada.*

* habits or repeated actions.
  *She **visits** her grandparents most weekends.*

Present continuous

Positive

I	**'m (am)**	talk**ing**.
He/She/It	**'s (is)**	
We/You/They	**'re (are)**	

Negative

I	**'m not (am not)**	talk**ing**.
He/She/It	**isn't (is not)**	
We/You/They	**aren't (are not)**	

Questions

Am	I	talk**ing**?
Is	he/she/it	
Are	we/you/they	

Short answers

Yes,	I	**am**.
	he/she/it	**is**.
	we/you/they	**are**.
No,	I	**'m not**.
	he/she/it	**isn't**.
	we/you/they	**aren't**.

We use the present continuous to talk about:

* actions that are happening now.
  *He**'s doing** his homework.*

* actions that are happening around now.
  *We**'re learning** to dance.*

Note: Look at the spelling changes:
cut – cutting   make – making

Present simple and Present continuous

We can contrast permanent activities (present simple) with activities happening now, today or around this time (present continuous).

*I**'m working** in Greece this summer but I **live** in York.*

Practice

1   **Choose the correct verb forms to complete the email.**

> **New Message**
>
> Hi Karen,
>
> Thanks for your email. Let me tell you something about myself.
>
> At the moment I **(a)** *sit* / *'m sitting* in my bedroom. I **(b)** *live* / *'m living* in a small village with my mum. I've got lots of friends but they **(c)** *aren't coming* / *don't come* here very often. We usually **(d)** *meet* / *are meeting* in town. Today it **(e)** *snows* / *'s snowing* outside, so I **(f)** *stay* / *'m staying* at home.
>
> What about you? **(g)** *Does it snow* / *Is it snowing* in Copenhagen at the moment too? What **(h)** *do you do* / *are you doing* when it snows?
>
> Speak soon,
>
> Hannah

Stative verbs

Stative verbs describe states, not actions. We don't usually use them in the continuous form. Some common stative verbs are:

*   verbs of being and owning, e.g. *be, have, own*
*   verbs of feeling or wanting, e.g. *hate, like, love, need, prefer, want, wish*
*   verbs of thinking, e.g. *agree, believe, know, remember, think, understand*
*   verbs that describe the senses, e.g. *feel, hear, smell, see, taste*
*   verbs that describe appearance and qualities, e.g. *appear, look* (= seem), *seem, sound*
*   other verbs, e.g. *cost, mean*.

Note: We can use some stative verbs in the continuous form when we describe actions, but the meaning is different.

He's having breakfast at the moment. (having = eating)

We're thinking about moving house. (thinking = considering)

Practice

2   **Choose the correct words to complete the sentences.**

a   *Do you like / Are you liking* playing computer games?

b   My father *doesn't know / isn't knowing* how to drive.

c   *Are you thinking / Do you think* it will rain later?

d   We *have / 're having* a meal. Do you want to join us?

e   Are you *seeing / looking at* the photos on your phone?

f   Sophie's *listening to / hearing* music in her room.

Adverbs of frequency, time phrases

We use adverbs of frequency to say how often something happens. Some common adverbs of frequency are: *always, usually, frequently, often, sometimes, occasionally, rarely, hardly ever, never.*

Adverbs of frequency come:

*   before main verbs.
    *I **never** watch TV.*
*   after *be*.
    *Harry **is always** late.*

*   after auxiliary and modal verbs.
    *We **have always** lived in Liverpool.*
    *You **must never** swim at this beach.*

Other time expressions usually go at the end of a sentence.

*We practise **twice a week**.*

Practice

1   **Write these words and phrases in the correct place in the table.**

> at the moment   every day   never
> now   often   on Fridays   once a year
> this week   today   usually

present simple	present continuous

2   **Choose six words or phrases from Exercise 1. Use them to write true sentences about you.**

Past simple

Positive

I/He/She/It/We/You/They	**watched** the film.

Negative

I/He/She/It/We/You/They	**didn't watch** the film.

Questions

Did	I/he/she/it/we/you/they	**watch** the film?

Short answers

Yes,	I/he/she/it/we/you/they	**did**.
No,	I/he/she/it/we/you/they	**didn't**.

We use the past simple to talk about:

*   an action that started and finished in the past.
    *Kyle **walked** home.*
*   two or more past actions that happened one after the another.
    *I **did** my homework and then **watched** TV.*
*   a past habit or regular past event.
    *Kate **worked** hard all year.*

Note: Look at the spelling changes:
*look – look**ed**   cure – cur**ed**   study – stud**ied**
shop – sho**pped***

Past continuous

Positive

I/He/She/It	**was**	talk**ing**.
We/You/They	**were**	

Negative

I/He/She/It	**wasn't**	talk**ing**.
We/You/They	**weren't**	

Questions

Was	I/he/she/it	talk**ing**?
Were	we/you/they	

Short answers

Yes,	I/he/she/it	**was**.
	we/you/they	**were**.
No,	I/he/she/it	**wasn't**.
	we/you/they	**weren't**.

We use the past continuous to:

- talk about an action in progress in the past.
  *I **was listening** to music.*
  *We **were cooking** a meal.*

- set the scene in a story.
  *I **was waiting** for my brother.*
  *We **were visiting** our grandparents.*

We use the past simple for an action that interrupts or happens during another action in progress in the past. For the action in progress, we use the past continuous.

*My mum **was living** in Hong Kong when she **met** my dad.*

We can use *while* instead of *when*, but we put *while* before the past continuous verb.

*The phone rang **while** I **was watching** a film.*

***When** the phone rang, I **was watching** a film.*

Practice

1 **Complete the sentences with the past simple form of the verbs in brackets.**

a Where .... (be) James yesterday?

b We .... (enjoy) the book more than the film.

c The film .... (not start) on time.

d I .... (see) that film last week.

e We .... (practise) every day for a month.

f The children .... (not want) to go out in the rain.

2 **Complete the sentences with the past continuous form of the verbs in brackets.**

a What .... (you/do) at this time last week?

b I .... (not live) in Hungary last year.

c .... (you/play) football when the teacher arrived?

d The internet .... (not work) yesterday, so we couldn't go online.

e Was the weather nice while .... (you/walk) yesterday?

f The television was on, but Sam .... (not pay) attention to it.

–*ing* form

We use the –*ing* form:

- as the subject or object of a sentence.
  ***Eating** vegetables is good for you.*
  *I really love **surfing**!*

- after prepositions.
  *I always end **up leaving** my keys at home.*
  *I went home **after finishing** my game.*

- after some verbs: *begin, continue, enjoy, finish, hate, like, love, imagine, practise, remember, start, stop, suggest.*
  *I **remember stopping** at the shop on the way home.*
  *I **continued playing** in the rain.*

Practice

1 **Complete the sentence with the correct form of these verbs.**

eat	look	paint	swim	talk	think

a .... is probably the best form of exercise.

b Thomas doesn't like .... in front of everyone else in class. He's very shy.

c My cousin didn't want to go to the zoo – she's not interested in .... at animals.

d After .... my lunch, I went round my friend's house and we played a video game.

e Without ...., Claire ran into the garden and rescued the bird.

f My dad finished .... my room yesterday. It looks great!

Will

Positive

I/He/She/It/We/You/They	'll (will)	win.

Negative

I/He/She/It/We/You/They	won't (will not)	win.

Questions

Will	I/he/she/it/we/you/they		win?

Short answers

Yes,	I/he/she/it/we/you/they	will.
No,	I/he/she/it/we/you/they	won't.

We use *will*:

- to talk about our personal ideas and opinions about the future.
  *Perhaps we **will use** e-books for all our studies in the future.*

- to make offers.
  *I**'ll help** you with your homework.*

- for unplanned decisions that we make at the time we are speaking.
  *I feel tired. I think I**'ll go** home now.*

Going to

Positive

I	'm (am)	going to	leave.
He/She/It	's (is)		
We/You/They	're (are)		

Negative

I	'm (am) not	going to	leave.
He/She/It	isn't (is not)		
We/You/They	aren't (are not)		

Questions

Am	I	going to	leave?
Is	he/she/it		
Are	we/you/they		

Short answers

Yes,	I	am.
	he/she/it	is.
	we/you/they	are.
No,	I	'm not.
	he/she/it	isn't.
	we/you/they	aren't.

We use *going to* to talk about:

- intentions and plans for the future that haven't been arranged or agreed yet.
  *I**'m going to visit** my friend in Turkey sometime next year.*

- things that we expect to happen because of outside information.
  *It**'s going to rain** soon. (There are big grey clouds.)*

Present continuous and Present simple

We use the present continuous for future arrangements. These are activities that we've agreed to do with other people. We know the details such as when, where, etc.

*I**'m playing** in a football match on Saturday.*

We use the present simple for schedules and timetabled events.

*The film **finishes** at 9:30 p.m.*

Practice

1 **Find and correct the mistakes with future forms in six of the sentences.**

a Oh look, there's no bread left. I'm going to the shop to get some.

b My friends go to the cinema later.

c I'm not sure why but I think the match tomorrow is being exciting.

d Do we play tennis after school?

e Ella's going to start school next year.

f Matt's listening to music later.

g The class starts at five on Friday.

h The flight arrives in a few moments.

2 Complete the sentences with the most appropriate future form of the verbs in brackets.

a I .... (meet) Simon at the theatre in ten minutes.

b I think Frank .... (be) tired tonight. He's been busy all day.

c The train .... (leave) at 3 p.m., so we've got an hour to get there.

d Tamsin .... (come) to visit me next week.

e Watch out! The dogs .... (jump) on you.

f The children want to go for a walk. I .... (take) them.

g Where .... (you/meet) William tomorrow?

h The play .... (start) at 7 p.m., so don't be late.

Advice

We use *should/shouldn't* + infinitive to give strong advice. This is an opinion about what we think is a good or bad idea.

*You **should have** a nap. You look tired.*

*You **shouldn't cycle** so fast.*

We use *should* in questions to ask for advice.

*What **should** I **do**?*

*Where **should** we **go** to get the bus?*

Suggestions

We use *how about* + noun/–ing, *why don't you/ we* + infinitive and *you could* + infinitive to make a suggestion. This is an idea for the listener to consider. We use *you could* + infinitive when different options are possible.

***How about watching** a film?*

***Why don't we go** out?*

*We **could go** by train to the beach or we could cycle.*

We use *shall I/we* + infinitive for suggestions and offers.

***Shall I bring** some crisps for the picnic?*

*What **shall we do** after school today?*

Practice

1 Complete the conversation with one word in each gap.

A: (a)............ we make a video today?

B: What about?

A: We (b)............ film ourselves on our skateboards.

B: Good idea. (c)............ don't we go to the skate park and film there?

A: Everyone does that. We (d)............ go somewhere different. It's better.

B: Alright. How (e)............ the beach? We could skate near the mini-golf course.

A: Sounds good. Shall (f)............ message Leanne and invite her?

B: OK … Done!

Present perfect

Positive

I/We/You/They	've (have)	started.
He/She/It	's (has)	

Negative

I/We/You/They	haven't (have not)	started.
He/She/It	hasn't (has not)	

Questions

Have	I/we/you/they	started?
Has	he/she/it	

Short answers

Yes,	I/we/you/they	have.
	he/she/it	has.
No,	I/we/you/they	haven't.
	he/she/it	hasn't.

We use the present perfect simple to talk about:

• something that happened at an unspecified time in the past.
We've met before.

• experiences.
She's climbed Mount Everest.

• something that happened in the past and has a result in the present.
Robert has broken his leg, so he can't play.

- a situation or an experience in our lives that is still true now.
  I've lived in this street all my life.

Present perfect with adverbs of time

We use *ever* in questions and statements to talk about whether an event or experience happened/didn't happen at some point in the past.

Have you ever lived in the USA?

We use *never* to talk about something that hasn't happened.

I've never eaten Japanese food.

We use *yet* in negative statements and questions to say whether something that was expected has happened.

I haven't finished my homework yet.

Has she found a job yet?

We use *just* for recent events.

I've just had a text from my friend.

We use *already* for something that has happened before now.

We're not hungry because we've already had lunch.

We often use *for* and *since* with the present perfect.

I haven't heard this song for years. (a period of time)

I've known Ian since I was seven. (a specific time in the past)

Practice

1 **Complete the sentences with the present perfect form of the verbs in brackets.**

   a Joe and I .... (buy) a ticket for the festival.

   b He .... (not do) his homework.

   c Harry .... (not eat) Japanese food before.

   d Which activities .... (you/try)?

   e .... (they/visit) their grandparents this year?

2 **Complete the sentences with *ever*, *never*, *yet*, *just* or *already*.**

   a Have you .... been to India?

   b I've .... been on holiday without my parents. I'd love to go alone!

   c Louise, have you found your phone ....?

d William didn't want to see the film because he's .... seen it.

e We've .... bought some pizzas for this evening. We got them a few minutes ago.

Past simple and Present perfect

We use the past simple for an action that happened at a definite time in the past.

I joined a chess club a few weeks ago.

We use the present perfect simple for a past action when we don't know when it happened, or when it isn't important.

We've visited this town before.

We also use the present perfect for something that happened in the past but in a period of time that is not finished, e.g. *today, this month*.

I've made a lot of new friends this year.

Practice

1 **Complete the conversation with the past simple or present perfect form of the verbs in brackets.**

   A: Everybody was talking about our video about freerunning at school this morning.

   B: Yeah, a boy from my football club **(a)**............... (text) me a few minutes ago. He says 250 people **(b)**............... (watch) it already. That's brilliant for the first day.

   A: I think we **(c)**............... (do) really well, don't you?

   B: Yes, it was a good idea. So lots of people **(d)**............... (see) the video. Do you think they liked it?

   A: Definitely! They **(e)**............... (leave) some really good comments. I think that before we **(f)**............... (make) the video, some people at school had the wrong idea about freerunning. They **(g)**............... (not think) it was a real sport.

   B: That's right. And now the video **(h)**............... (show) everyone how good we are!

Zero conditional

if clause	main clause
if/when + **present simple**	**main verb** + **present simple**
When I **meet** my sister,	we often **talk** for hours.

We use the zero conditional to talk about something that always or usually happens.

If/When my friend sings, everyone stops to listen.

I don't watch TV if/when I have homework.

First conditional

if clause	main clause
if + **present tense**	*will/could/might* + **infinitive**
If you **like** action,	you**'ll enjoy** this film.

We use the first conditional to talk about a possible action in the future.

If you don't understand the words, you could look them up online.

If I have time at the weekend, I might practise that new song.

Practice

1 **Complete the zero and first conditional sentences with the correct form of the verbs in brackets.**

a When mum .... (see) her friends, they always .... (talk) about work.

b If you .... (meet) Jack today, you .... (be able) to tell him about the party.

c You .... (not get) any better if you .... (not practise).

d If I .... (become) rich, I .... (buy) a huge house!

e When you .... (press) this key on the piano, it .... (make) a very deep sound.

f Dad .... (not come) to the play if it .... (start) in the afternoon.

g When Richard .... (not have to) go to school, he never .... (get up) early.

h If you .... (ask) Mum nicely, I'm sure she .... (help) you.

Second conditional

if clause	main clause
if + **past simple**	*would* + **infinitive**
If I **became** a film star,	I **would go** and live in Hollywood.

We use the second conditional:

* to talk about imaginary or unreal situations in the present.
  If I were a good singer, I would be in a famous pop group.
  If my dog could talk, he'd ask me to feed him more often!

* to talk about present or future situations that are possible but unlikely.
  If I won lots of money, I'd buy more musical instruments for my school.
  If I met my favourite actor, I would ask him how he got where he is now.

* to give advice.
  If I were you, I'd have extra music lessons.
  I would work harder at school if I were you.

Practice

1 **Make second conditional sentences.**

a if / he / not stay up so late, he / not feel tired in the morning

b if / I / have / enough money, I / buy / a new shirt

c if / she / not like / you, she / not invite / you / to all her parties

d if / we / have / some food, we / make / lunch

e if / he / be / more careful, he / not make / so many mistakes

f if / you / lie / to me, I / be / very angry

Unless, in case, if I were you

Unless

We can use *unless* instead of *if not*.

I can't help you if you don't tell me your problem.

I can't help you unless you tell me your problem.

If he doesn't pass his music exam, Sam won't be happy.

Unless he passes his music exam, Sam won't be happy.

Note: We don't use a negative verb after *unless*.

Unless you ~~don't invite~~ invite him, he won't come to the party.

In case

We can use (*just*) *in case* instead of *if* when we want to stress 'to be safe or prepared'.

I'll take my coat (just) in case it gets cold.

I always have my phone (just) in case I need to call someone.

If I were you

We can use *if I were you* to give someone advice. We use it in second conditional sentences.

If I were you, I would change football teams.

I'd take my coat if I were you. It's freezing outside!

Practice

1   Complete the sentences with *unless* or *in case*.

a   The boys won't come .... you want them to.

b   Maria bought tickets early .... they sold out.

c   I won't watch you .... it makes you nervous.

d   You won't survive in show business .... you have contacts

e   Miriam won't go on stage .... her mum goes with her.

f   I'll stay with Leo .... his parents are late.

Present simple passive

subject +	be (am/is/are) +	+ past participle (+ by)	
The river	is	cleaned	every year.
The bottles	aren't	used	again.
The articles	are	written by the students.	

Past simple passive

subject +	be (was/were) +	+ past participle (+ by)	
The trees	were	destroyed by the fire.	
The caves	were	found by a tourist.	
The book	was	published	in 2017.

We use the present simple passive or past simple passive:

•   when we want to focus on the action more than the person that does or did the action.
*The old clothes **are recycled**.*
*The bridge **was repaired**.*

•   when we don't know or don't want to say who does or did the action, or when it's obvious who did it.
*The film **was watched** around the world.*
*My phone **was stolen** at the train station.*

When we know or want to mention who does or did the action, we use *by*.

*The island was discovered **by a famous scientist**.*

Verbs without an object (e.g. *come, go, happen, arrive*) are not used in the passive because there is no object to become the subject.

Note: When we form the passive, it is important to make sure we use the correct form of *be*. To do this, look at the subject and think about whether it is singular or plural.

***The pizza was** delivered by someone on a bike.*

***Pizzas were** invented in Italy.*

Practice

1 Complete the sentences with the present simple or past simple passive form of these verbs.

clean	collect	deliver	drive	film
give	make	speak	steal	waste

a A parcel .... for you yesterday.

b Some jewellery .... from a house yesterday.

c English .... all around the world.

d Tonnes of water .... every day when people leave taps running.

e These chocolates .... by hand in Switzerland last week.

f The movie .... in a castle in Wales.

g Ben and Fiona .... to school by their mum every morning.

h A large amount of rubbish .... from the beach last week.

i The office .... every day by a team of cleaners.

j Homework .... to students each day.

2 Complete the text with the correct active or passive form of the verbs in brackets.

Forest food

Last week I **(a)**.................... (take) to an amazing restaurant for my friend's birthday. It's called The Green Forest Café and it **(b)**....................
(locate) in a forest about thirty kilometres from my town. My friend's dad drove us to a car park nearby and then we **(c)**.................... (walk) for about half an hour through the trees to get to the café.

The building **(d)**.................... (make) from wood. It has large windows and a glass ceiling, so you really feel part of the forest around you. The food is delicious. The salad and vegetables **(e)**.................... (grow) locally and they **(f)**....................
(freshly/pick) every day. We **(g)**....................
(serve) our meal by a really friendly waiter, who **(h)**.................... (explain) some of the things we could see around us. It was really interesting. We all enjoyed the experience a lot.

Have/Get something done

subject +	*have/ get* +	object +	past participle	
Present simple				
We	have	our pool	cleaned	every week.
I	get	my hair	cut	at Headlines.
Past simple				
She	had	her photo	taken	for her passport.
I	got	my teeth	checked	last week.

We use *have/get something done* when somebody else does something for us. We often pay them to do it for us. *Get something done* means the same as *have something done,* but it is less formal. We use it when we are talking.

I ***get my make-up done*** by Selina.

When we want to say who does the action for us, we use *by*.

*He had his room decorated **by a professional**.*

Practice

1 Complete the sentences with the present or past simple form of *have/get something done.*

a I .... (have; repair / my computer) yesterday.

b We .... (get; deliver / our post) every day at about 11 a.m.

c Kate .... (get; cut / her hair) last weekend.

d Bob .... (have; wash / his car) every week.

e They .... (have; clean / the offices) four times a week.

f My grandmother .... (have; paint / this portrait) twenty years ago.

g I .... (get; fix / my camera) today.

h We .... (have; paint / the boat) every two years.

Defining relative clauses

That's the girl	**who/that**	wants to be a pilot.
The train	**which/that**	leaves in ten minutes is full.
That's the place	**where**	we need to meet.
That's the boy	**whose**	bike was stolen.

We use defining relative clauses to describe exactly which people, things, places, etc. we mean. We use:

- *who* or *that* for people
- *which* or *that* for things/animals
- *where* for places
- *whose* to show possession.

Defining relative clauses can give us information about the subject or the object of the main clause. We often use them to join two sentences.

A girl found my passport. (A girl is the subject.)

She was very nice.

*The girl **who found** my passport was very nice.*

*I met **a girl** yesterday. (A girl is the object.)*

She speaks four languages.

*The girl **who I met** yesterday speaks four languages.*

We can leave out the relative pronoun when it is the object of the relative clause.

*The girl **I met** yesterday speaks four languages.*

We don't use commas in defining relative clauses.

We use *whose* as the possessive form of *who*.

*This is Ella, **whose** family I travelled with last summer.*

Practice

1 Choose the correct words to complete the sentences.

a Is that the woman *which / who* won the dance competition?

b The singer *that / which* I like watching most on stage is Lady Gaga.

c The bands *which / who* we saw at the festival were great.

d I'd like to find a flight *that / who* goes direct.

e Do you know the name of the song *which / where* is playing now?

f There are some beaches *where / who* it's dangerous to swim.

g That's the man *which / who* I saw when at the station.

h The boy *which / who* sat next to me on the train came from Russia.

2 Circle the relative pronoun if it is not necessary.

a The town where we stayed was really expensive.

b The girl who I sat next to at school is famous now.

c The website which you recommended was really useful.

d We went to a restaurant where you had to cook your own food!

e The girls thanked the man who gave them directions.

f Is that the short story which you said won the competition?

Modals of obligation, prohibition and necessity

Present

must	I **must get** a new passport.
	You **mustn't use** a mobile phone on the plane.
have to	We **have to collect** the tickets from the station.
	He **has to stay** here.
	They **don't have to leave** now.
	She **doesn't have to pay** for her ticket.
	Do we **have to go** now?
	Does he **have to be** here?

Past

had to	I was late, so I **had to run** to the bus stop.
	We **didn't have to walk** because the bus came.
	Did you **have to buy** another ticket?

Future

will have to	We**'ll have to go** home soon.
	You **won't have to talk** to him again.
	Will she **have to find** a different flight?

We use *must* when we think it is very important or necessary to do something.

I **must buy** a new bag for the journey.

We use *mustn't* when it's important or necessary not to do something or when something is prohibited.

You **mustn't tell** him about the party.

We use *have to* to talk about something that is important or necessary, often because it's a general rule.

All passengers **have to show** their passports before they get on the plane.

We use *don't have to* to talk about something that isn't necessary or when there is no obligation.

You **don't have to sit** there if you don't want to.

We use *had to* to talk about obligation in the past.

I **had to buy** another ticket.

We use *will have to* to talk about obligation in the future.

You**'ll have to take** the bus to the airport.

Need to

We use *need to/don't need to* when we think something is/isn't necessary but not an obligation.

We **need to see** our grandparents before we leave.

Practice

1 **Choose the correct words to complete the sentences.**

   a We *have to / need to* wear a tie at school. It's a rule.

   b We *mustn't / needn't* wear trainers. They're not allowed.

   c We *had to / must* give in our homework yesterday.

   d You *don't need to / mustn't* bring a ruler. I've got one.

   e Next week we *will have to / must* practise the play.

   f You *don't need to / mustn't* join the football team. It's up to you.

2 **Complete the text below with the correct form of *have to*, *must* or *need to*.**

My advice for a school trip

On our last school trip we went to Rome and I learnt a lot about travelling. Here's some helpful advice for what to do when you are on a school trip.

- You **(a)**_____ look after all your money. Ask the group leaders to hold it for you.
- Normally, you **(b)**_____ allow for ten euros a day but you don't **(c)**_____ take more than this.
- At the airport you'll **(d)**_____ collect your luggage and take it to check-in. Nobody will do it for you and the check-in staff **(e)**_____ know it's your luggage.
- You **(f)**_____ write you flight number down so you're sure you're in the right place at the right time.
- You **(g)**_____ leave your luggage anywhere. Make sure it's always with you.
- You **(h)**_____ keep your passport with you at all times. Put is somewhere safe. Make sure no one can take it.

Reported speech – statements

direct speech	reported speech
'I **take** photos of the stars.'	Liam said (that) he **took** photos of the stars.
'I **can** see it.'	Elena said (that) she **could** see it.
'I **will** do it again.'	Nathan said (that) he **would** do it again.

We use reported speech to tell somebody else what a person said.

Liam said (that) he read about the stars every night.

In reported speech, the main verb usually moves back one tense into the past.

She said, 'I **want** to be a dancer.'

She said (that) she **wanted** to be a dancer.

Practice

1   Rewrite the statements in reported speech.

a   'I love playing guitar,' said Manuel.

....

b   Lexi said, 'I'll call you later.'

....

c   Alec said, 'I'm starting a new project.'

....

d   'I can't come to your party,' Rene told Sandra.

....

e   'The bus will leave soon,' Mum told Jake.

....

Reported speech – questions

Yes/No questions

direct speech	reported speech
She asked me, '**Are** you **studying** Arabic?'	She asked **if** I **was studying** Arabic.
She asked me, '**Do** you **live** in London?	She asked me **if** I **lived** in London.

When we report *yes/no* questions, the verb is not in question form and we don't use the auxiliary verb. We use *if* instead.

Wh- questions

direct speech	reported speech
She asked me, '**What's** your name?'	She asked me **what** my name **was**.'

When we report *wh-* questions, the verb is not in question form – we use the same structure as in statements. We repeat the question word in the reported question.

We use *say* or *tell* when reporting statements. *Tell* needs an object.

Adam said, 'I love photography.'

*Adam **said** (that) he loved photography.*

Lizzie told the receptionist, 'I need to collect a form.'

*Lizzie **told the receptionist** (that) she needed to collect a form.*

We use *ask* in reported questions. We can use it with or without an object.

'What happened?' he asked.

*He **asked** what had happened.*

'Where are you?' she asked me.

*She **asked me** where I was.*

Practice

2   Rewrite the reported questions as direct speech.

a   Jane asked what I was cooking.

....

b   Ben asked if we were finished.

....

c   Our teacher asked if we could help her.

....

d   Greta asked if I had seen Piotr.

....

e   The tour guide asked what we wanted to do next.

....

Pronouns in reported speech

In reported speech, we change subject pronouns (*I, you, he, she*, etc.), possessive pronouns (*mine, yours, his, hers*, etc.) and possessive adjectives (*my, your, his, her*, etc.) so that it's clear who or what they refer to.

*Sandra said, '**My** hobby is collecting shells.'*

*Sandra told me (that) **her** hobby was collecting shells.*

Practice

3   Complete the sentences with the correct pronouns and possessive adjectives.

a   'You need to come back later,' the woman told him.

The woman said that .... needed to come back later.

b   'We need to leave,' said the man.

The man said that .... needed to leave.

c   'Your brother is my best friend,' William told me.

William said that .... brother was .... best friend.

d   'I've got your book,' my friend told me.

My friend told .... that .... had .... book.

Indirect questions

Yes/No questions

direct question	indirect question
Is it a difficult job?	**Can you tell me if it's** a difficult job?
Do they live here?	**Do you know if they live** here?

Wh- questions

direct question	indirect question
Where do you practise?	Can you tell me where you practise?
Why do you enjoy your hobby?	Can I ask why you enjoy your hobby?

In indirect questions, we use the same verb form as in statements – the verb is not in question form.

In *yes/no* questions, we use *if*. In *wh-* questions we use the question word.

Does he work here?

*Can you tell me if **he works** here?*

*What time **does the concert start**?*

*Do you know what time **the concert starts**?*

Practice

1   Choose the correct words to complete the sentences.

    a   Fay asked *when / if* I was cold.

    b   Michiko asked *which / if* coat was mine.

    c   Lynn asked *what / if* I liked watching sport.

    d   Delia asked *what / if* I was having for dinner.

    e   Simon asked *where / if* I went at the weekend.

    f   James asked *where / if* I could help him.

Past perfect

Positive

I/You/He/She/It/We/They	'd (had)	finished.

Negative

I/You/He/She/It/We/They	hadn't (had not)	finished.

Questions

Had	I/you/he/she/it/we/they	finished?

Short answers

Yes,	I/you/he/she/it/we/they	had.
No,		hadn't.

We use the past perfect to talk about something that was completed at an earlier point in the past.

*I got a lovely surprise on my birthday. My parents **had organised** a party.*

Practice

1   Find and correct the mistakes in six of the sentences.

    a   I had stay up too late, so I didn't want to get up early.

    b   My mum chose a film that we already seen.

    c   I couldn't read what I'd wrote in my notebook.

    d   I couldn't call him because I left my phone at home.

    e   I was hungry this evening. I missed lunch.

    f   After we'd finished lunch, we carried on shopping.

    g   School closed early because the heating break down.

    h   Theo's phone had no battery because he'd forgotten to charge it.

Past perfect and Past simple

We use the past perfect with the past simple to show that one action happened before another in the past. The past perfect describes the first action, the past simple the second.

past			now
	✕	✕	
	*The party **had** finished*	*when Ben arrived*.	

(First, the party finished. Then, Ben arrived.)

We can also say:

*When Ben **arrived**, the party **had finished**.*

We use many of the same time expressions that we use with the present perfect. We use adverbs of time, e.g. *already*, *ever*, *just* and *never*.

*She offered us a snack but we'd **just** had lunch.*

*Mark was funny. I'd **never** met anyone quite like him.*

*I didn't want any more surprises. I'd **already** had enough!*

We use time linkers (e.g. *after*, *before*, *by*, *once*, *until*, *when*) to talk about two actions in the same sentence.

After they had seen the concert, they went to bed.

By the time we got to school, the first lesson had started.

Once it stopped raining, we went for a walk.

My parents had left for work **when** *I got up.*

Practice

1   Complete the text with the past simple or past perfect form of the verbs in brackets.

A bad start to the day

Sarah decided to take the bus to school. Her dad's car **(a)**.................. (break down) the day before, so he couldn't take her.

She **(b)**.............. (just/get) there when the bus arrived. She got on and **(c)**.............. (reach) into her bag to get her purse. That was when she realised she **(d)**.............. (leave) it at home.

Walking was her only option but it was raining and she **(e)**.............. (not/bring) an umbrella. Still, she started to walk. After a few minutes, a car **(f)**.............. (drive) past her really fast and **(g)**.............. (hit) a huge puddle. The water **(h)** ....(fly) up in the air and **(i)**.............. (land) on Sarah. She looked like she **(j)**.............. (just/ get) out of the bath!

Used to

Positive

I/You/He/She/It/We/They	**used to**	**collect** comics.

Negative

I/You/He/She/It/We/They/	**didn't use to**	**have** any hobbies.

Questions

Did	I/you/he/she/it/we/they	**use to**	**have** any hobbies?

We use *used to* to talk about something that happened regularly in the past, but does not happen now. We use it to refer to past habits or states.

He **used to enjoy** drama at school, but he doesn't do it now.

I **didn't use to watch** horror films, but I like them now.

You speak French well. **Did** you **use to live** in France?

We often use *used to* with *never*.

I **never used to like** curry but I do now.

Jack **never used to be** so tall.

We don't use *used to*:

* to talk about an action which happened only once or twice
* with a time expression that tells us how many times an action happened
* with a time expression that tells us when an action happened.

I ~~used to swim~~ **swam** in the sea a few times when I was young.

We ~~used to go~~ **went** swimming last August.

We don't use *used to* to say how long a **state** lasted. But we can use it to talk about how long a repeated or regular past **action** lasted.

They ~~used to live~~ **lived** here for ten years.

I ~~used to like~~ **liked** this song for about two years but I don't now.

We **used to play** in the tree house for hours.

She **used to practise** singing for two hours a day.

Practice

1   Complete the sentences with the correct form of *used to*.

a   I .... (not) like running but I love it now.

b   .... (you) go to the cinema often when you were young?

c   Agata .... read comics but now she reads novels.

d   .... (you) live with your grandparents?

e   Victoria .... work abroad every summer but she doesn't now.

f   .... (your sister) have curly hair?

g   Stan .... (not) say much in class but he's much chattier these days.

h   I .... (not) be interested in maths but now I quite like it.

SPEAKING BANK

Part 1 Phases 1 and 2

In Phase 1 of Part 1, you answer simple questions about your name, your age, where you live and who you live with. In Phase 2 you answer one or two more questions on personal topics, such as your hobbies, home life, daily routine, likes and dislikes, and so on.

Exam help

- ✔ Phase 1 questions are always the same. Practise answering them clearly and confidently.
- ✔ You only need to give short answers in Phase 1.
- ✔ Give longer answers in Phase 2. Explain and give reasons for your answer.
- ✔ Some questions begin with the words 'Tell us about …'. Say as much as you can about the topic.
- ✔ Think about the tense: the question may be about the present, the past or the future.
- ✔ If you don't understand a question, ask the examiner to repeat it.

Useful language

Giving personal information

My name's …
I'm … years old.
I live in the city centre.
I live in a city/town/village called …
There are … people in my family.
I live with my parents …
I have … brothers and sisters.
My … also lives with us.
I go to school in …

Likes and dislikes

I like/prefer … because …
The … I like best is … because …
My favourite … is … because …
I don't like … because …
I don't really enjoy … although I have to do it at school.
I'm not keen on …
I prefer …
I'd rather do … than …
What I like about … is … because …

Practice Part 1

1 Complete the sentences with information about yourself.

- **a** My name's …
- **b** I'm … years old.
- **c** I live in …
- **d** I live with …
- **e** My favourite sport is … because …
- **f** In the evenings I like … because …
- **g** Last year, I went to … on holiday. It was fun because …
- **h** After school I usually …

2 Read the statements and add a reason. Use a verb and words from the box, or your own ideas.

> clever lyrics   cold weather   Italian food
> get on well / sisters   videos and podcasts
> with a team

- **a** I love pasta because …
- **b** I'm not keen on skiing because …
- **c** I like spending time at home because …
- **d** What I like about football is …
- **e** I don't like studying from books, I'd rather …
- **f** My favourite music is rap because …

In this part of the test, you speak on your own for about one minute. You describe a photograph. Remember that your photograph is on a different topic from your partner's.

Exam help

- ✓ Begin by talking about the general situation, then talk about the people.
- ✓ Use the present tense to talk about what you can see.
- ✓ Talk about the people, their appearance, clothes, feelings and so on.
- ✓ Use the present continuous to talk about what people are doing.
- ✓ Talk about the objects, the weather, the things you see in the background.
- ✓ Use your own ideas about the photograph and say why you think that.
- ✓ Use other words to say what you want or move on to a different part of the photo.

Useful language

Talking about the photograph
In the foreground, there are some teenagers who are …
In the background, I can see some people who are …
Behind the people, I can see …

Talking about the people
He's about … years old.
She's got long blonde/dark hair.
He's carrying a …
They're wearing …

Talking about what people are doing
She's doing her homework.
They're eating breakfast.
He's playing the guitar.

Talking about the place
She's sitting in her bedroom.
It's a nice room with large windows.
There are lots of people in the shopping mall.
The weather is hot and sunny.

Giving your own ideas
I think they look very happy.
They don't seem very interested in …
It looks like the weekend because …
Perhaps they're brother and sister, or maybe they're just friends.

When you're not sure of the word
I don't know the word in English, but you … with it.
It looks like a …, but it's bigger.
I don't know what it's called but you keep … in it.
It's the place where you …

Practice Part 2

1   **Choose the correct word to complete the sentences describing people.**

   a   The boy's wearing his school *clothes* / *dress*.

   b   I think they're the same family because they *look* / *see* very similar.

   c   The girl's got long dark *hair* / *hairs,* but the boy's is blond.

   d   Both boys are *carrying* / *holding* books in their schoolbags.

   e   The boy's concentrating *hard* / *much* on his homework.

   f   The girl's *doing* / *playing* tennis, and she's enjoying it.

   g   The four friends are talking to *every* / *each* other in the café.

   h   I think it's the boy's birthday because I can see a big cake *in* / *on* the table.

2   **Choose the word from the box for the thing each student is describing.**

   | cash desk   helmet   kettle   necklace |
   | oven   remote control |

   a   It's a device you use to change the channel on the TV.

   b   It's a pretty thing you wear round your neck.

   c   It's the thing in the kitchen you use to bake bread and cakes.

   d   You use one for boiling water when you make hot drinks.

   e   It's the place where you pay for something in a shop.

   f   You wear one on your head when you go cycling.

3   **How would you describe these things if you couldn't remember the word?**

   a   a bookcase

   b   a sofa

   c   a games console

   d   a belt

   e   a pair of scissors

   f   traffic lights

Part 3

In this part of the test, you discuss a task with your partner. You can start by talking about the different options in turn, and responding to each other's comments.

Exam help

- ✓ The examiner describes the situation and tells you and your partner what to discuss.
- ✓ The task has a title to help you remember what to talk about.
- ✓ Look at the page of pictures. The picture in the middle tells you the situation.
- ✓ Remember, you have to talk to your partner in this part.
- ✓ Decide who's going to begin and which picture to talk about first.
- ✓ Talk about the people in the situation, not about yourselves.
- ✓ Say whether each idea is good or not for the people in the situation. Give reasons.
- ✓ Listen to your partner and say what you think of his/her ideas.
- ✓ Talk about all the ideas in the pictures before you decide which is best/most useful/most enjoyable.

Useful language

Getting started

Where shall we start/begin?
Let's start with this one. Is this a good … ?

Asking for opinions

What do you think of this idea?
I'm not sure about … What do you think?
Do you think … would be a good idea for them?
What about … ?

Explaining opinions

I think a … is a good prize because …
In my opinion, … is a good idea because …
I think they should buy … because …
I don't think … is a good idea because …

Agreeing

I agree.
That's true/right/what I think too.
That's a good point.
Exactly!

Disagreeing

Maybe that's not such a good idea because …
I'm not sure about that because …
I don't agree with you really because …
Sorry, I don't think so.

Moving on

Let's talk about this activity next.
Okay, but what about … ?
So which one do you think is best?
What shall we choose then?
Let's choose the …

Practice Part 3

1 **Two students are discussing a Part 3 task. What is student B doing in each conversation? Write the correct letter: A agreeing, D disagreeing, O giving an opinion, R giving a reason, T changing the topic.**

a A: I think a box of chocolates would be a good prize.

B: Really? I'm not sure about that.

b A: Why do you think a teddy bear is a good gift for the teacher?

B: Because everybody likes teddy bears.

c A: What do you think about the family having a barbecue in the garden?

B: I think that could be a good idea if the weather is good.

d A: Why don't you like the idea of the girl going to the cinema?

B: Well, it's not a good way to make new friends because you can't talk to them there.

e A: If the family go sightseeing in the city, they can talk about it afterwards.

B: I see what you mean – that's true actually.

f A: What about ice-skating?

B: I really think the whole family would enjoy that.

2 **Put the words in the correct order to make sentences from a discussion.**

a start / this / with / let's / activity / .

b do / this / what / think / you / idea / of / ?

c what / that's / think / I / too / .

d I / agree / we're / think / going / to / don't / that / about / idea / !

e that's / I'm / good / not / a / activity / young / for / children / sure / .

f I / with / really / you / don't / I / because / think / that's / don't / very / agree / useful.

g point / a / that's / good / .

h will / do / which / activity / you / the / family / all / think / enjoy / ?

Part 4

In this part of the test, the examiner asks you questions about the topic of Part 3.

Exam help

- ✓ The questions are on the same topic as Part 3, but the questions are more general, they're not about that situation.
- ✓ Talk about your own personal experiences and opinions.
- ✓ The examiner may ask a question to you directly, or may ask a question for either of you to answer.
- ✓ Listen to what your partner says because the examiner may ask you if you agree, or ask what you think about the same question.

Useful language

Giving yourself time to think

That's a difficult question – let me think for a moment.

Sorry, I don't understand. Could you say that again, please?

Sorry, I've forgotten the question. Could you repeat it, please?

Giving personal opinions

For me, the most important thing is …

In my opinion, the most interesting … is/are …

If you ask me, the best thing is …

I think the main reason for … is to …

Giving examples

For example, …

Let me give you an example, …

I think a good example of that is when …

Agreeing and disagreeing with what your partner says

I agree with … when he/she says … because

That's what I think too because …

I partly agree with that idea, but …

I don't agree with that really because …

To be honest, I'm not sure about that because …

Practice Part 4

1 Match the students' answers (A–F) to a reason (i–vi).

A If you ask me, it's important to do homework because …

B In my opinion, it's much nicer to relax in the sun on a beach when you're on holiday, although …

C I prefer watching sport to doing it – …

D People need to stay healthy but they don't need to do sport , for example …

E I love spending time with my friends so …

F I don't do anything with my friends at the end of the day because …

i that's the best thing in my opinion.

ii I'm usually at home with my family.

iii you can learn more about what you've done in your lessons.

iv I know some people like skiing, so they prefer cold places.

v I'm not very good at team sports!

vi they could just eat healthy food.

2 Now match the examiner's questions to the students' answers in Activity 1. There is one extra answer you don't need to use.

a Do you prefer going on holiday in hot or cold places?

b Is it a good idea for everyone to do a sport?

c What do you usually do in the evenings with friends?

d Do you think everyone should do homework every day?

e What's the best thing about being at school?

3 Complete the students' answers with the words and phrases in the box.

| honest | in fact | let me | moment | opinion |
| rather | repeat | seems | | |

a Well, I'd … play a sport like football than tennis because I love taking part in team games.

b In my … the school day is too long and the holidays are too short! I like having a lot of free time in the summer.

c I hate doing homework – … , I think we have to do too much! I usually spend two hours doing it every evening.

d To be … , I don't like reading books very much, although I do sometimes read a book after I've seen the film.

e I think live music is great – … give you an example of a concert I went to.

f It … to me that it's important to eat healthy food as well as doing exercise if you want to keep fit.

g Sorry, I didn't understand. Could you … the question, please?

h I need to think about that for a … – it's a difficult question.

WRITING BANK

Part 1: Email

In this part of the test, you have to reply to an email that has been sent to you. You do this using four notes written on the email.

Sample answer

See Writing Part 1 Test 1 task on page 25.

See Writing Part 1 Test 1 task on page 25.

New Message

Hi Max

How are you? Your brother told me that you really like tennis actually. He said that you watch it on TV all the time. ◄··········· *this is about the first note, with reasons*

I could go on Sunday instead of Saturday. Would that be good for you too? ◄··········· *this is about the second note*

You can wear any kind of shorts and T-shirt that you want at the club, but you need to make sure that you wear proper tennis shoes. You can't just play in trainers! ◄··········· *this is about the third note*

use informal punctuation such as exclamation marks

I'd love to go for something to eat afterwards but there are no restaurants or cafés near the club. Why don't we go into town and find somewhere to eat there? ◄··········· *this is about the last note*

I'm really looking forward to it! ◄··········· *make a suggestion*

Love

Marek

add a comment to make your email more personal

Useful language

Starting an email
Hi …
How are you?
Great to hear from you.

Saying thank you
That meal you cooked for me was great!
Please thank your brother for …
Thank you so much for …

Making a suggestion
Maybe we can go for a swim in the morning.
Why don't we … ?
I think it would be a good idea to …
I think we should …
Let's …

Explaining or giving reasons
I was so busy that I forgot to …
I don't eat … because it's bad for me.
I prefer to … because …

Inviting
Would you like to … ?
It would be great if you could come.

Finishing an email
Have a great weekend!
Please write to me soon.
See you next week!
Love …

Exam help

- Read the email from your friend carefully.
- Read the notes one by one and, for each note, underline the important words in the email. Underlining the key words will remind you that you must write something about all the notes.
- Start with a friendly, informal greeting.
- Write complete sentences and check that you're using the correct form of verbs (present, past or future).
- Don't be afraid to use some interesting vocabulary and expressions you know.
- Make sure you write about 100 words. Try not to write fewer than 90.
- When you've finished, check your email for spelling and grammar mistakes.

Practice Part 1: Email

1 **What are the problems with this email? Think about:**

grammar   spelling

number of words   replies to all notes.

New Message

Hi Max,

Your brother says me that you like playing the tennis, that's why I know.

You must to wear tennis shoes – normal trainers is no good. About the clothes, you can shorts and a T-shirt or a tracksiut – it's your choose. Near the club there aren't a restaurant or café.

I hope that you enjoy playing tennis.

Marek

---

2 **Correct the grammar and spelling mistakes in the email in Activity 1.**

3 **Complete each sentence with the best linking word from the box. Use each word only once.**

and   because   but   if   when

a I enjoy walking in the countryside .... looking around cities too.

b I love swimming .... it really helps me to relax.

c I'll send you a message tomorrow .... my train is delayed.

d I wrote to my friend .... she didn't reply.

e We can have lunch .... we start to feel hungry.

4 **Read the statements and add a reason. Write a different reason for each sentence.**

a I can't play football today because …

b I love going to the cinema because …

c I don't often watch documentaries because …

d I visit my grandparents every week because …

e I don't like eating at restaurants because …

f I enjoy going to museums because …

Planning your answer

Aim to write several paragraphs, not just one long paragraph.

Starting an email

- Don't forget to put an informal greeting (*Hi Max*).
- It can sound strange if you start the email by responding to the first note immediately, so start your email with a sentence such as *How are you?* or *Thanks for your email*.
- The first paragraph should also contain your response to the first note.

Middle paragraphs

- These should contain your responses to the other three notes.
- If one of the responses is very short, you can put responses to two notes into a single paragraph. This will help you avoid having a paragraph containing only one sentence.

Finishing your email

- Don't forget to add a comment (*I'm really looking forward to it!*).
- Include a way of saying goodbye (*Love / Bye for now / See you soon*).
- Put your name at the bottom.

How to use the written notes

Each note will be only a few words long. Decide what kind of information you need to include in your response to each one (a reason, explanation, saying thank you, etc.), then think of what you could say.

Make sure you include as much information as you can for the longer responses, when you have to explain or give reasons. Very short responses will not get good marks!

Make sure you respond to all four notes. You will lose marks if you don't. When you've finished writing, check carefully that you have clear responses to all four notes.

Checklist

When you finish writing a short message, use this checklist:

○ **Content**
Have you responded to all four notes?

○ **Communicative achievement**
You are writing to a friend, so have you used an informal friendly style?

○ **Organisation**
Have you included a suitable greeting?
Have you divided your writing into paragraphs?
Have you ended your email in a suitable way?
Have you put your name at the bottom?

○ **Language**
Have you used the correct tenses?
Have you used a range of vocabulary?
Have you checked your spelling and punctuation?

In this part of the test, you can choose to write an article about a topic of interest. You do this using some questions that are presented in an advertisement or an announcement.

Sample answer
See Writing Part 2 Test 1 task on page 27.

Learning a language

Is the best way to learn a language by going to classes or by going to a country where the language is spoken? Whatever method you choose, it takes lots of time and practice.

You can't really learn a language well just by going on holiday somewhere because it isn't long enough. If you live there for several months, though, you'll use the language every day and will improve very quickly.

If this isn't possible, then learning in class with a teacher will help. However, you will probably only practise for two or three hours a week. Therefore, learning a language in this way will take much longer.

Use the title that is in the task.

You can start with a question, which you will then answer.

Don't be afraid to give your opinions.

Words like 'However' and 'Therefore' help you organise the points you must include.

This is your answer to the question about whether it's better to have classes with a teacher.

Finish with a sentence that briefly mentions what you have already said.

Exam help

- ✓ Read the question very carefully.
- ✓ You must answer one question, 'What's the best way to learn a language?', but this is split into two parts. The first part is 'Is it better to have classes with a teacher?' The second is 'Is it better to go to a country where they speak the language?' You must also explain your opinions ('Why?').
- ✓ Underline the sentences in the sample answer that answer the first part of the question.
- ✓ Underline the sentences in the sample answer that answer the second part of the question.
- ✓ Write down some of your own opinions about this topic, then think of the reasons for your opinions.
- ✓ Try to enjoy writing the article and remember your readers should enjoy it too!
- ✓ When you've finished, make sure you've written about 100 words and check your article for spelling and grammar mistakes.

Useful language

Starting the article
Do you think/agree that … ?
Have you ever thought about … ?
Is the best way to learn by going to classes?

Giving your opinion
I think/believe that …
In my opinion, …
You can't/shouldn't …

Talking about cause and result
If you live there … you'll use the language
If this isn't possible, then learning in class will help.
This isn't possible so …

Explaining or giving reasons
Therefore …
That's why …
For this reason …

Adding information
However, …
Also, …

Imagining things
What would happen if … ?
People/You could try …

Finishing your article
Therefore I think …
For these reasons I think…

Practice Part 2: Article

1 Discuss with a partner. Think about the points in the box.

> A magazine has lots of articles. Some look interesting, some don't. What makes you want to start reading one of the articles?

Interesting information?   Good title?
Seems fun to read?   Interesting first line?

2 You can make an article more interesting by starting with a question. Match the article titles (i–iii) with the questions (A–E). There are two questions you do not need.

i Making new friends

ii The importance of friends

iii How to help a good friend

A Do we really need friends in our lives?

B Should we tell our new friends all our secrets?

C How can we make new friends?

D How do we communicate with our friends?

E What can we do when a friend needs us?

3 You can also make an article more interesting by giving personal opinions. Join these sentences to express an opinion. Use the words in the box.

| after   but   for example   if   so |

a You may not agree with me .... I think some teenagers hate hobbies.

b I'm sure that hobbies help teenagers relax .... they've had a difficult day at school.

c There are lots of reasons for having a hobby, ... making new friends, developing new skills, etc.

d Young people are very sociable .... they like having hobbies they can share with friends.

e Many people have no time for hobbies .... they're at work all day.

4 Look at the topics below. Think of two or three questions you might ask about this topic.

Give your questions to a partner, and look at the questions they give you.

Try to write responses, with reasons, to each of your partner's questions. Then compare your work with your partner.

Topics:
- festivals in your country
- giving presents
- helping the environment
- the town or city where you live.

Planning your answer

Aim to write several paragraphs, not just one long paragraph.

Starting your article

Use a question at the beginning of the first paragraph, which you then provide a short answer to in the next sentence.

Middle paragraphs

These should contain your answers to the questions that are asked in the announcement or notice. Remember to give reasons as well as your opinions. This should mean that each paragraph is several sentences, not just one. You should aim to write one paragraph for each of the questions in the task.

Ending your article

You need a conclusion, which is usually a summary of the opinions you gave in your article. This should come at the end of the final paragraph.

Checklist

When you finish writing a short message, use this checklist:

Content
Have you answered all of the questions in the task?
Have you added reasons to your opinions?

Communicative achievement
The article is for readers of a magazine or a website who you don't know, so have you used a suitable semi-formal style?

Organisation
Have you included a suitable introduction?
Have you divided your writing into paragraphs?
Have you included a suitable conclusion?

Language
Have you used the correct tenses?
Have you used a range of vocabulary?
Have you checked your spelling and punctuation?

Part 2: Story

In this part of the test, you can choose to write a story. You are given the first sentence of the story and you have to continue the story for about 100 words.

Sample answer
See Writing Part 2 Test 1 task on page 27.

As they set off on their bikes, they knew they were going to have an exciting day. Andrew and Richard had loads of things to eat and drink and games to play too because they were going to spend a day at the beach. But what exciting things would happen?

When they arrived, they started playing football. Richard accidentally kicked the ball into the sea and ran in to get it. Just as he got into the water, three dolphins, which seemed to want to play with the ball, suddenly appeared near him.

Andrew went into the water too and they started throwing the ball around. The dolphins were swimming after the ball – it was amazing. Fortunately, they took some photos so everyone would believe their story.

Use linking words such as 'because' to join your ideas.

Add excitement to your story by using questions like this.

Use different verbs to describe what happened.

It's a good idea to write some longer sentences using linking words like 'who' or 'which'.

You can say what the friends did, or what the friends thought, to add interest to your story.

This is a good sentence to finish your story.

Exam help

- ✓ Do not change the first sentence of the story.
- ✓ If the sentence is about a person, make sure your story is all about him/her.
- ✓ Divide your story into three paragraphs so that it is clear to the reader.
- ✓ Make your story interesting by using a range of vocabulary and expressions.
- ✓ Check your grammar, particularly all your verb tenses.
- ✓ As well as telling the events of the story, you can add in what the people were thinking and/ or what they said.
- ✓ When you've finished, make sure you've written about 100 words, and check your story for spelling and grammar mistakes.

Useful language

In a story,

- You need verbs in the past tense (e.g. *were playing, ran, had seen, kicked*) because stories happen in the past.

- You will get better marks if you use different past tenses, e.g. past simple, past continuous, past perfect.

- You need to use words that link the actions in the past (e.g. *after that, later, when*) to make your story easy to follow.

- You need a variety of adjectives, adverbs and other words and phrases (e.g. *exciting, frightened, scared, surprised, suddenly, unexpectedly, before he had time to say anything*) to add interest and excitement to your story.

- Try to use words which mean the same (synonyms) instead of repeating the same word (e.g. *nice/lovely/beautiful/*etc.).

Practice Part 2: Story

1 **Choose the word that fit best in each space.**

> dangerous   decided   didn't have
> had   left   said   sat   scared   stupid
> Suddenly   took   walked   was   were

It was getting late, so Peter **(1)**............... to
go home. He **(2)**............... goodbye to his
friend and **(3)**............... to the bus stop. There
(4)............... only a few people in the street
because it **(5)**............... almost eight o'clock
in the evening, but he wasn't **(6)**............... or
anything. The town wasn't a **(7)**............... place.
Peter **(8)**............... on a seat and **(9)**...............
his phone out of his back pocket. **(10)**...............,
he realised that he **(11)**............... his rucksack
with him. He had **(12)**............... it at his friend's
house! He felt really **(13)**...............!

2 **How did the people feel? Complete the
sentences with adjectives from the box.
More than one adjective may fit into some
of the gaps.**

> awful   confident   confused   delighted
> disappointed   frightened   interested
> shocked   surprised   terrible

a Tom felt so .... that he couldn't
move.

b Emma was .... to see her old
friend after so many years.

c Martin was .... to find his
computer in the wrong place.

d Clare was .... when she heard her
friend wouldn't be able to come.

e Sally felt very .... that she would
win the tennis match.

f During his illness, George felt ....,
but he recovered quickly.

g What's the answer to this question? I'm
really ....

h Clare was .... to hear that Mark
had had an accident. What ....
news!

i Justine wasn't .... in reading the
poem I wrote.

3 **Try writing the first sentence of a story.**

Give your sentence to a partner and look at the
sentence that they give you.

Think of some ideas for a story that continues
this first sentence and make some notes.

Take turns telling each other your story.

Planning your answer

Aim to write several paragraphs, not just one long paragraph.

Starting your story

Make sure that you have at least one more sentence in the
first paragraph after the sentence you are given. This should
include any background information you need to give, for
example, about the people or the place, and the first part of
the story.

Continuing your story

The middle section should contain the main part of the
story and may be split into two paragraphs if necessary.
Remember to add details to your story. This should mean
that each paragraph is several sentences, not just one.

Ending your story

The final part of the story should include a sentence at the
end that finishes the story in an entertaining way.

Checklist

When you finish writing a short message, use this
checklist:

Content
Does your story have a beginning, a middle and an
end?
Have you added details and language to make the
story more interesting to read?

Communicative achievement
The story is for people who are reading for pleasure,
so have you used a suitable entertaining style?

Organisation
Have you divided your writing into paragraphs?
Have you included suitable linking words and phrases
to join the parts of your story together?

Language
Have you used the correct tenses?
Have you used a range of vocabulary?
Have you checked your spelling and punctuation?

VISUALS FOR SPEAKING TESTS

Part 2 Candidate A

Photograph 1A

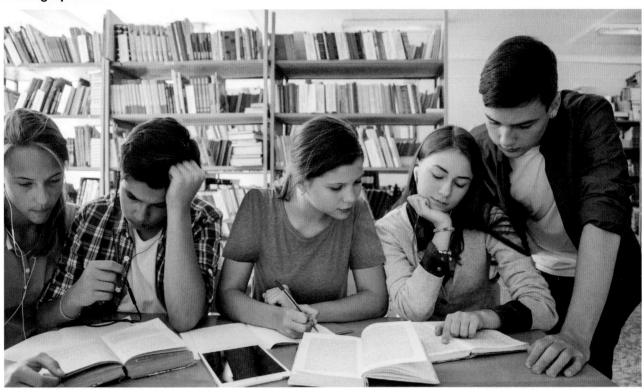

Photograph 2A

Photograph 3A

Photograph 4A

Part 2 Candidate A

Photograph 5A

Photograph 6A

VISUALS FOR SPEAKING TESTS

Photograph 7A

Photograph 8A

Part 2 Candidate B

Photograph 1B

Photograph 2B

Photograph 3B

Photograph 4B

Photograph 5B

Photograph 6B

Photograph 7B

Photograph 8B

A new hobby

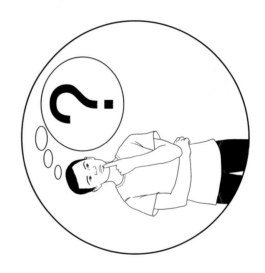

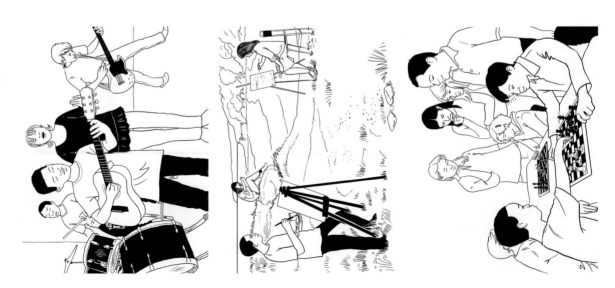

A new apartment

Activities for a girl's fourteenth birthday

Gift for a teacher who's retiring

Activities to do with a friend who's won an important race

A long bus journey

Activity for the last day of the school year

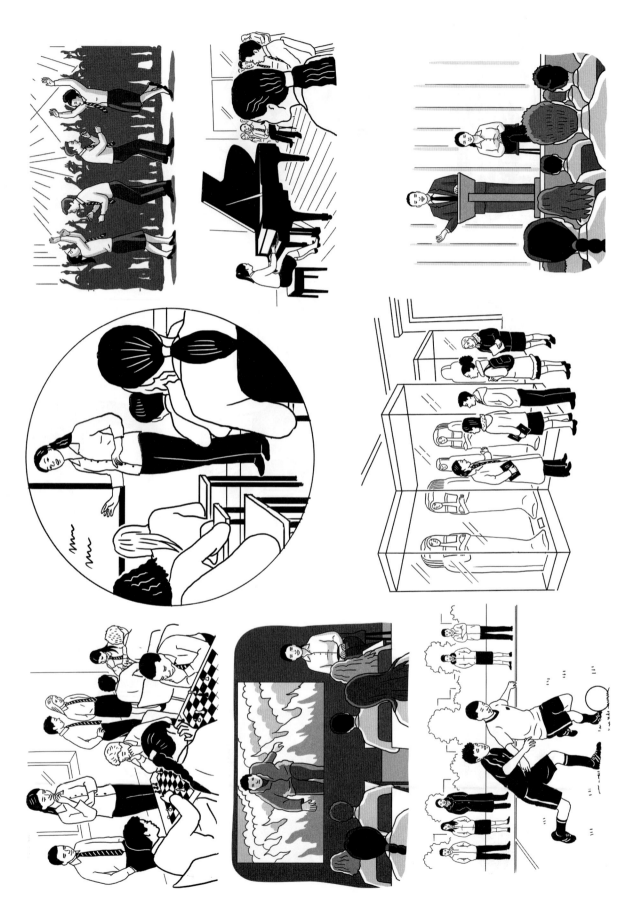

Gifts for young customers from a new computer games shop

PRELIMINARY FOR SCHOOLS GENERAL QUESTIONS

1 How many marks are needed to pass the exam?
➤ To pass the exam with a grade C, you need around 60 percent of the total marks.

2 Do I have to pass each paper in order to pass the exam?
➤ No. Each paper doesn't have a pass or fail mark. Your overall grade comes from adding your marks on all four papers together.

3 Are marks taken off for wrong answers?
➤ No. This means that, if you're not sure, you should always try to guess – you might be right.

4 Am I allowed to use a dictionary in the exam?
➤ No, this is not allowed during the exam.

5 In Writing Part 1 what happens if I don't write about all the points listed?
➤ You should write about all the things the task requires. The examiners are looking to see if you can provide the right information and good language.

6 In Writing Parts 1 and 2, what happens if I write too few or too many words?
➤ The word count is an important guide. It tells you how much to write to complete the task. But don't waste time counting every word – just make sure you use about the right number.

7 Generally, in the exam, if I'm not sure about an answer, can I give two possible answers?
➤ No. If there are two answers, and one of them is wrong, you will not get a mark. So you must decide on one answer to give.

8 In Writing Part 1, do contractions count as one word or two?
➤ Two. For example, mustn't = must + not = two words.

9 What happens if I make a spelling mistake in the Writing Parts?
➤ Spelling is one of several things the examiner considers when deciding what mark to give you. Check your spelling as much as possible.

10 What happens if I make a spelling mistake in Listening Part 3?
➤ It depends. If the examiner can still easily understand what word you meant to write, you will get the mark.

11 How many times will I hear each recording in the Listening paper?
➤ You will hear each recording twice.

12 In Listening Part 3, should I use the words I hear in the recording or is it better to use different words?
➤ You must write only words (or numbers) that you actually hear in the recording. Also, you must not change these words.

13 In Listening Part 3, what happens if my answer is too long to fit in the space on the answer sheet?
➤ Most answers are one or two words or a number. These answers will easily fit in the spaces on the answer sheet. If your answer is longer than this, it is probably either wrong, or you are including too much.

14 In the Speaking test, can I take the test alone? Or can I choose my partner?
➤ You must take the Speaking test with a partner. This is because your ability to discuss things with another student is an important part of what is tested.

15 For the Speaking test, is it a good idea to prepare what I'm going to say in Part 1?
➤ It is, of course, good to prepare well for the exam. But you cannot know exactly what the examiner will ask beforehand, so you must listen very carefully to the examiner, and make sure you answer the questions relevantly.

16 In the Speaking test, what if my partner makes a lot of mistakes, or doesn't talk much or talks too much?
➤ Don't worry about these things. The examiner will make sure you have a fair chance in every situation.